my first
knitting
book

my first knitting book

35 easy and fun knitting projects
for children aged 7 years +

CICO kidz

Published in 2013 by CICO Kidz
An imprint of Ryland Peters & Small
519 Broadway, 5th Floor, New York NY 10012
20–21 Jockey's Fields, London WC1R 4BW
www.rylandpeters.com

10 9 8 7 6 5 4 3 2

A CIP catalog record for this book is available from
the Library of Congress and the British Library.

ISBN: 978-1-78249-039-5

Printed in China

Editor: Katie Hardwicke
Designer: Barbara Zuñiga
Step artworks: Rachel Boulton
Animal artworks: Hannah George
Photographer: Emma Mitchell, Terry Benson,
Martin Norris and Penny Wincer
For further credits, see page 128.

Contents

Introduction 6

Materials   8

Techniques   9

CHAPTER 1   20
COZY KNITS

Cowl   22

Earmuffs   24

Little bear hat   28

Fingerless mitts   32

Rainbow earflap hat   34

Animal scarves   36

Panda hat   38

Pompom scarf   42

Octopus hat   44

Mouse mittens   48

Monster hat   51

CHAPTER 2   54
STYLISH KNITS

Little bows   56

Legwarmers   58

Decorative buttons   60

MP3 or phone cover   62

Pompom necklace   64

Ballet slippers   67

Tassel belt   70

Heart key ring charm   73

Pencil case   76

CHAPTER 3   80
HOME KNITS

Hot-water bottle cover   82

Patchwork blanket   84

Heart pillow   88

Caterpillar doorstop   90

Zigzag pillow   94

Toy basket   97

CHAPTER 4   100
FUN KNITS

Sheriff's star badge   102

Ladybug buddies   104

Doctor's stethoscope   106

Baby ball   108

Teddy bear   110

Pirate flag   114

Cute alien   117

Rag doll   120

Templates   124

Suppliers   126

Index   128

Acknowledgments   128

Introduction

Knitting used to be for grannies—not any more! With the bright, exciting projects in this book everyone will want to get knitting. And once you've started, you'll want to take your knitting anywhere and everywhere—after all, you only need two needles and a ball of yarn to knit.

The basic knitting stitches are easy to learn, especially if you ask your granny or your mom to help get you started. Once you have mastered these, there is no limit to the different projects you can make and in this book we have 4 different chapters to inspire and challenge you. Cozy Knits is full of crazy hats, scarves, and mittens that will keep you warm and make you laugh. Stylish Knits are just that—projects to make pretty accessories to add style to any outfit. In Home Knits you can find patterns to make pillows and doorstops and other items to brighten up your room or give as gifts. Finally, in Fun Knits, you'll find cuddly toys, from a cute teddy to a crazy alien, along with a pirate flag and sheriff's badge for the dressing-up box.

Most of the projects are very easy, but to help you know where to start, we have graded them with one, two, or three smiley faces. Projects with one smiley face are based on simple rectangles. You will need to cast on and knit but won't have any complicated decreasing or increasing to do. (There is even one project—the pompom necklace—that only uses finger knitting!) Two smiley faces mean that the project is slightly harder and you will use some simple shaping involving increasing and decreasing, and follow a knitting pattern line by line. Those projects with three smiley faces are for when you are becoming something of an expert and can follow a more challenging pattern, using new stitches and techniques.

We have included a techniques section, which explains all the different techniques you will need to finish each project, from how to cast on stitches to how to sew on buttons. Each of the abbreviations that are used in the knitting patterns is explained here with diagrams to show you exactly what to do. Good luck with your knitting adventure!

Project levels

Level 1

These are quick, easy projects that use basic knitting stitches.

Level 2

These projects take a little longer and use more advanced techniques and some sewing.

Level 3

These projects may have several stages and require more difficult knitting and sewing techniques.

Materials

You need just two items to start knitting: a pair of needles and some yarn. There are a also few other bits and pieces that you'll need to make some of the projects in this book, but none of them are expensive and you'll probably have some of them at home already.

- **Knitting needles**
  Needles come in different materials and sizes. Each pattern tells you the size you will need to make the project.

- **Pompom maker**
  These little gadgets offer a quick and easy way to make pompom embellishments (or you can use cardboard rings).

- **French knitting bobbin**
  These come with instructions on how to make knitted cords.

- **Stitch holder**
  These look like giant safety pins and are used for the more complicated projects where you need to separate some stitches to work on later.

- **Buttons**
  Use buttons to add decoration or fastenings to your knitting.

- **Scissors**
  Always cut your yarn, don't break it, even when the pattern says "break yarn," as strong yarn will cut your hand.

- **Sewing needle and thread**
  For sewing on buttons and stitching felt or fabric to your knitting.

- **Darning needle**
  These are large, blunt needles with big eyes that can be threaded with yarn for sewing up your knitting.

- **Crochet hook**
  This is useful for picking up dropped stitches or making crochet chains.

- **Pins**
  Thick pins are best for holding bits of knitting or fabric together when you sew them up.

- **Scraps of fabric**
  Keep a sewing basket with scraps of fabric, felt, ribbons, and trimmings close by you to help finish some of the projects and add your own personal touch.

- **Fiberfill toy stuffing**
  For turning your knitted items into soft toys or filling out shapes.

YARNS
The projects give you the brand and type of yarn we used but if you can't find an exact match you will still be able to knit using a similar type of yarn. For example, if the pattern uses an Aran weight yarn, any type of Aran yarn can be substituted.

When you buy yarn, you can find what type it is on the ball label. The label will also tell you what needle size to use.

Knitting Techniques

Getting Started

Holding the yarn and needles

There is no one correct way to hold the yarn and needles, everyone finds their own comfortable position, but if you follow these suggestions, you will find it easier to keep an even gauge (tension) when knitting.

There are two most common ways of holding the needles: like a pen or like a knife.

You can hold each needle in the same way, or have each hand use a different way.

Remember that even if you are left-handed you can knit like this, as both hands do some work.

Holding the yarn

The ball end of the yarn is wrapped around the right-hand little finger in order to control the amount and speed of yarn feeding through from the ball, and so to control the gauge (tension) of the work (see page 13). The yarn then passes under the two middle fingers and over the pointy finger, which helps to "flick" the yarn around the needle as you knit. If this is too hard at first, you can simply grip the yarn with the right hand and "throw" it round the needle.

Slip knot

The first step when starting to knit is to make a slip knot, which will also be your first stitch. When you are knitting, the yarn leading to the ball is called the "ball-end" of the yarn.

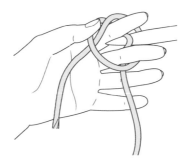

Wind the yarn once around two fingers and then over the two fingers again behind the first loop (closer to your hand). Use a knitting needle to pick up the back of the second loop you made and pull it through the front loop to make a slip knot on the needle.

Casting on

There are many ways to cast on, but for beginners this is the simplest way, so use this to start with—you can progress to something harder once you have mastered knitting.

1 Make a slip knot on the needle and pull on the ends of the yarn to make the slip knot tight on the needle. You have made your first stitch.

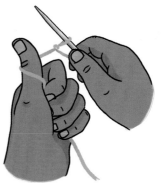

2 Holding the needle in your right hand, make a loop around your left thumb with the ball-end of the yarn.

3 Slip the needle under the loop. Remove your thumb and pull the stitch tight on the needle. Add on as many stitches as you need in the same way.

Knitting stitches

Once you have cast on, there are only two stitches in knitting, knit stitch and purl stitch: so there isn't very much to learn!

The aim is to hold the needle with the stitches on in your left hand and the empty needle in your right hand, and to transfer all stitches onto the right-hand needle by knitting a row.

Knit stitch

This is the simplest of all stitches.

1 Hold the needle with the cast-on stitches in your left hand. Insert the tip of the right-hand needle into the first stitch on the left-hand needle, from the left side of the stitch so that you are going from the front to the back of the knitting. Holding the ball-end of the yarn at the back of the knitting, wrap this yarn around the point of the right-hand needle with your right hand, passing the yarn underneath then over the point of the right-hand needle.

2 With the tip of the right needle, pull the yarn through the stitch on the left-hand needle to form a loop. This loop is your new stitch.

3 Slip the loop off the left-hand needle to complete the stitch, which is now on your right-hand needle.

Repeat these steps with each stitch, until all the stitches on the left-hand needle have been knitted and transferred to the right-hand needle. This completes the row. To start a new row, swap the needles in your hands so that the needle with the stitches is in your left hand and the yarn is in position at the start of the row.

Purl stitch

This stitch is almost as simple as knit stitch. Most of purl stitch is the other way around to knit stitch. You still hold the needle with stitches in your left hand, but you insert the right-hand needle a different way into each stitch and you hold the yarn at the front.

1 Hold the needle with the cast-on stitches in your left hand. Insert the tip of the right-hand needle into the first stitch on the left-hand needle, from the right side of the stitch so that you are going from the back to the front of the knitting. Holding the ball-end of the yarn at the front of the knitting, wrap this yarn around the point of the right-hand needle with your right hand, passing the yarn over and around the right-hand needle.

2 With the tip of the right needle, pull the yarn through the stitch on the left-hand needle to form a loop.

3 Slip the loop off the left-hand needle to complete the stitch, which is now on your right-hand needle.

Repeat these steps with each stitch, until all the stitches on the left-hand needle have been transferred to the right-hand needle. This completes the row. To start a new row, swap the needles in your hands so that the needle with the stitches is in your left hand and the yarn is in position at the start of the row.

Bind (cast) off and fastening off

When you have finished knitting you need to bind (cast) off so that your work doesn't just unravel!

1 First knit two stitches (see page 10). Slip the tip of your left-hand needle into the first stitch knitted, lift it over the stitch closest to the tip of the needle and drop it off the needle. Be careful that the other stitch stays on the needle. Knit one more stitch onto the right-hand needle

again, and repeat until all you have left is one stitch on the right-hand needle. All the other stitches have been bound (cast) off.

2 Slip the last stitch off the needle, pull it out a bit to make it bigger, then cut off the yarn, leaving a long tail. Slip the tail through the loop of the last stitch then pull on the tail to tighten the loop and finish the bind (cast) off. This is called fastening off.

Binding (casting) off in rib

You can also bind (cast) off in rib if you have been using that stitch for the fabric, as it will give you a neat and stretchy edge.

To do this, cast (bind) off as normal, simply working across the stitches in the rib pattern (knit 1, purl 1) you have been working, rather than knitting all of them.

1 Work 1 knit stitch and 1 purl stitch. Take the yarn to the back. Slip the tip of your left-hand needle into the first stitch you knitted and lift it over the stitch closest to the tip of the needle and drop it off the needle.

2 Knit the next stitch then pass the purl stitch over and off the needle as before.

3 Bring the yarn to the front (as if to purl) and purl the next stitch. Repeat steps 2 and 3 along the row until you have one stitch left. Fasten off.

Stitch patterns

Depending on how you combine knit and purl stitches, you can make various stitch patterns to produce knitted fabrics that feel and look very different.

Garter stitch

Knitting every row forms a ridged fabric called garter stitch, which is the simplest stitch pattern. It is the same on both sides and so is a flat, even fabric that is perfect for scarves or edges.

Stockinette (stocking) stitch

This is made by alternately working one row of knit stitch and one row of purl stitch. This makes a fabric that is different on each side. The knit, or plain, side is flat and the stitches look like little "V"s. The purl side is bumpy and textured, with the stitches like little wiggles and is called reverse stockinette (stocking) stitch.

This fabric curls slightly and so is best used in projects that need to be sewn up, which flattens the curly edges.

Seed (moss) stitch

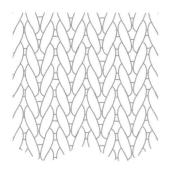

Seed (moss) stitch is made by working alternate knit and purl stitches across the same row. As you hold the yarn at the back for knit stitches and at the front for purl stitches, you need to move it after each stitch.

After a knit stitch you must pass the yarn in between the needles to the front of the knitting to work the next purl stitch. After a purl stitch you must pass the yarn in between the needles to the back to make the next knit stitch.

In each row you knit the stitches that were knitted in the last row, and purl those that were purled to create the bumpy texture.

Rib stitch

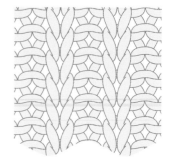

Rib stitch is created like seed (moss) stitch by working knits and purls alternately across a row. But in each row you knit the stitches that were purled in the last row and vice versa to make the vertical stripes of stitches.

Gauge (tension)

Everybody tends to knit at a different gauge (tension), which depends on how big or small your stitches are, how loosely or tightly you knit, and what needles and wool you use. The gauge will affect how big your knitting turns out.

For most of the patterns in this book you do not have to worry about gauge as it doesn't really matter how big or small the final project is. However, when you are getting really good at knitting and begin trying some of the Level 3 hat patterns, gauge does matter because your finished hat could be too big or too small if it is wrong.

So, before you begin your project you need to knit a gauge (tension) swatch. This is a small square about 4 x 4in (10 x 10cm) in the main yarn and stitch used in the pattern. Lay the swatch flat, place a ruler on it, and count the number of stitches per inch (or centimeter).

If you find you have more stitches per inch (or centimeter) than asked for in the pattern, then your gauge is too tight and you need to make it looser. The best way to do this is to try a bigger size of knitting needle. Knit another swatch and check again. Increase the size of the needle you use until the gauge is as close as you can get it to the one you need for the pattern. If there are fewer stitches than asked for in the pattern, then your gauge is too loose, and you need to use smaller knitting needles.

Shaping

To shape a knitted piece you have to increase or decrease the number of stitches on the needles. Here are the simplest ways:

Increasing (inc1)
This is also known as knitting twice into a stitch, or knit into front and back.

1 Knit into the front of the next stitch on the left-hand needle in the normal way, but do not slip it off the needle. With the stitch still on the left-hand needle and the yarn at the back, knit into the back of the same stitch and then slip it off the needle.

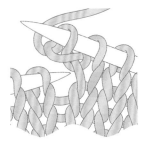

2 You have made one stitch into two stitches and so increased by one.

Decreasing: knit 2 stitches together (k2tog)

1 Instead of inserting your right-hand needle into the front of the first stitch on the left hand needle, insert it into the second stitch and then into the first stitch as well.

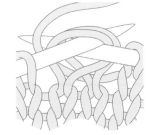

2 Then knit the two stitches together (see page 10), and slide both from the left-hand needle. You have made two stitches into one and so decreased by one.

Purl 2 stitches together (p2tog)
Simply insert your needle through 2 stitches instead of one when you begin your stitch and then purl them (see page 10) in the normal way.

Slip slip knit (ssk)

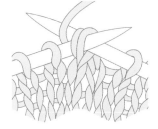

This is another way of decreasing. Slip one stitch and then the next stitch onto your right-hand needle without knitting them. Then insert the left-hand needle from left to right through the front loops of both the slipped stitches and knit them as normal (see page 10).

Changing color or joining a new ball

When you want to make striped fabrics, or you run out of a ball of yarn, you need to add a new ball, or the next color, at the beginning of the row.

Tie the new yarn around the tail of the old yarn, keeping the knot loose. Push the knot up next to stitches then pull it tight. Work the next row using the new yarn.

Picking up stitches

Sometimes you need to work a neat edge along the side of a fabric you have already knitted. To do this you need to pick up stitches to knit all along the edge. Always do this with the right side of the fabric facing you and try to space the stitches you pick up at equal intervals.

1 Hold the needle in your right hand and insert it through the fabric from front to back where you want to pick up the stitch. Wrap a new piece of yarn around the needle, as if to knit a stitch.

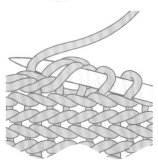

2 Pull the loop through the knitted fabric to the front. Continue in this way along the edge until all the stitches are picked up. Work on these stitches as instructed in the pattern.

Picking up dropped stitches

Sometimes a stitch will accidentally slip off your needle before it is knitted and will create a space, or a ladder, in your knitting. You can pick up the dropped stitch using a crochet hook.

1 With the knitting facing you, knit to where there is a gap left by the dropped stitch. Insert a crochet hook from the front to the back through the dropped stitch and hook it behind the strand of the "ladder" above it. Pull the ladder through the stitch with the hook. Keep hooking the ladders until you reach the top, then slip the loop onto the left-hand needle, and knit it as normal.

Weaving in yarn ends

When you have finished a piece of knitting (especially a stripy one) you will have lots of untidy tails of yarn loose at the edges. It is important to weave these into your knitting to make it tidy and secure. You can't just cut them off or your knitting will unravel. Always weave in any ends when you have finished your knitting.

To weave them in, thread a darning needle with one of the tails of yarn. On the wrong side, take the needle through the knitting one stitch down on the edge, then weave it through the stitches, without letting your needle go through to the right side, working in a gentle zigzag. Work through 4 or 5 stitches then return in the opposite direction. Remove the needle, pull the knitting gently to stretch it, and trim the end.

Sewing up

Sewing up knitting can be done in many ways, but using overstitch is the easiest. For each method thread a darning needle with a long piece of yarn.

Overstitch

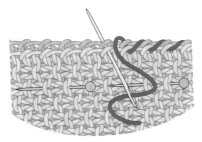

Secure the yarn to one piece of fabric with a few little stitches on the back. Lay the pieces to be joined with right sides together. Insert the needle into the front of one piece of fabric then through to the back of the adjoining fabric. Bring the yarn over the top of the edges ready for the next stitch. Repeat all along the seam.

You can see the overstitch stitches quite easily so sometimes it is nice to make a feature of this by using a different color yarn to the one used in the project.

Flat seam

This is the technique used for sewing the back seams on the hats. It creates a join that is completely flat.

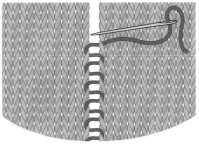

1 Lay the two edges to be joined side by side, right sides up. Pick up the very outermost strand of knitting from one side and then the other, working your way along the seam and pulling the yarn up firmly every few stitches.

Other knitting ideas

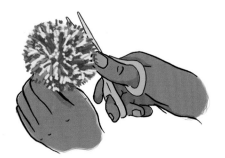

Making pompoms

1 Decide the size of your finished pompom. Find a round object with the same diameter and draw around it twice onto a piece of stiff cardstock. Draw a smaller circle inside each larger one (draw around a large button or a cotton reel) exactly in the middle. Cut out the larger circle then cut out the inner circle to make two donut shaped rings.

2 Hold the 2 rings together and wrap the yarn around them and through the center hole, wrapping it closely together. Don't wrap too tightly or it will be difficult to cut. When there are lots of layers of yarn all around the ring, and there is no center hole left, carefully push the point of a pair of scissors through the yarn between the two layers of cardstock. Snip through the layers of yarn all around the ring.

Slide a length of yarn between the cardstock rings and tie it tightly with a knot to hold all the strands together. Leave the end of this piece of yarn long for attaching to your projects.

3 Pull off the cardstock rings (you can reuse them for your next pompom) and fluff up the pompom. You can trim any straggly ends with scissors to make a neat ball.

Finger knitting

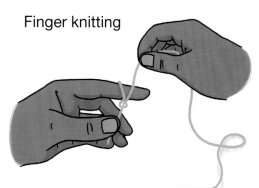

1 Make a slip knot in the yarn and slip it over your pointy/forefinger of the hand that you don't write with (so, the left finger if you are right-handed). Wrap another loop of yarn over your finger, closer to the end.

2 Holding the long end still with your second finger and thumb, with your right hand pull the first loop over the top of the second loop so you have one loop left on your finger.

3 Pull your finger up to tighten the loop that has just come off. Then pull the end of the yarn to tighten the loop which is still around your finger—you'll soon get the hang of it. Put another loop over your finger and do it all again. Keep going until your chain is long enough, then slip the last loop off your finger, push the end of the yarn through the loop, and pull tight. Leave the yarn end long.

French knitting

When you buy a French knitting kit, or knitting nancy, it will come with instructions. Here are a few guidelines to help get you started:

1 Thread your yarn through the center hole and twist the yarn around the prongs in a counter clockwise direction, as shown.

2 When all the prongs are wrapped, make another loop over one prong, pick up the bottom loop with the hook and lift it over the top loop and the prong. Wrap the yarn over the next prong and then lift the bottom loop over the top and the prong. Repeat round. A cord of knitting will start to appear through the bottom of the spool.

3 To finish, simply cut the yarn and thread the end through the loop on each prong, then pull tight.

Finishing Touches

------------Sewing buttons

Buttons make great decorations for all sorts of projects.

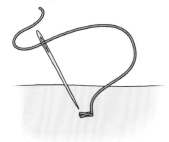

1 Mark the place where you want the button to go. Push the needle up from the back of the fabric and sew a few stitches over and over in this place.

2 Now bring the needle up through one of the holes in the button. Push the needle back down through the second hole and through the fabric. Bring it back up through the first hole. Repeat this five or six times. If there are four holes in the button, use all four of them to make a cross pattern. Make sure that you keep the stitches close together under the middle of the button.

3 Finish with a few small stitches over and over on the back of the fabric and then trim the thread.

Embroidery Stitches

Running stitch

This is the simplest stitch and can be used in embroidery and for joining two layers of fabric together.

Secure the end of the thread with a few small stitches. Push the needle down through the fabric a little way along, then bring it back up through the fabric a little further along. Repeat to form a row of wide stitches.

Cross stitch

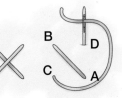

Knot your thread, bring the needle up at A and down at B, then up at C and down at D. Knot again at the back or come up in the position of the next cross.

Backstitch

This is a very useful stitch, since it is strong and similar to the stitches used on a sewing machine. It makes a solid line of stitches.

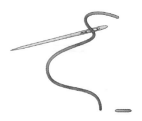

1 Start as if you were sewing running stitch. Sew one stitch and bring the needle back up to start the second stitch.

2 This time, instead of going forward, go back and push the needle through at the end of your first stitch.

3 Bring it out again a stitch length past the thread. Keep going to make an even line of stitches with no gaps.

Chain stitch

This stitch is a pretty stitch to learn, you can use it for details on the animal hats.

Bring the needle out at the end of the stitching line. Re-insert it at the same point and bring it out a short distance away, looping the thread around the needle tip. Pull the thread through. To begin the next stitch, insert the needle at the point at which it last emerged, just inside the loop of the previous chain, and bring it out a short distance away, again looping the thread around the needle tip. Repeat to continue.

French knot

These little stitches are great for adding pupils to eyes.

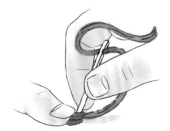

Bring the needle up from the back to the front. Wrap the thread two or three times around the tip of the needle, then reinsert the needle at the point where it first emerged, holding the wrapped threads with the thumbnail of your non-stitching hand, and pull the needle all the way through. The wraps will form a knot on the surface of the fabric.

Blanket Stitch

This makes a pretty edge when you are sewing two layers of knitting together, or as a decorative edge on a piece of felt.

1 Bring the needle through from the back to the front at the edge of the fabric. Push the needle back through the fabric a short distance from the edge and bring the tip up above the edge of the fabric. Loop the thread under the needle. Pull the needle and thread as far as you can to make the first stitch.

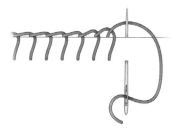

2 Make another stitch to the right of this and again loop the thread under the needle. Continue along the fabric and finish with a few small stitches or a knot on the underside.

Following a knitting pattern

To make some of the projects in this book you will need to follow the patterns. These give instructions on how many and what type of stitches you need. Knitting patterns use abbreviations for the stitches, such as K for knit and P for purl. Patterns combine different numbers of stitches and, sometimes, different types of stitches, to make the shape of the knitted piece.

Knitting patterns are written out as instructions, one row at a time. Start by casting on the number of stitches required and then work each row—remember, your slip knot counts as your first stitch. To help you to keep track of where you are, tick off each row with a pencil when you have completed it. Sometimes the pattern will include the number of stitches that you have made at the end of each row, shown in brackets. Check that your stitches match.

First, practice the basic stitches, how to join in new colors, and how to fasten off, by making a few rectangles of knitting. Once you feel happy that you can work all the different types of stitches, you will be ready to start on your very own project.

Finishing your project will involve some different techniques, from weaving in ends, to sewing up the pieces and sewing on buttons or attaching pompoms. You'll find instructions on how to do this with each project.

Abbreviations

cm	centimeter
dec	decreas(e)(ing)
g	grams
in	inch
inc	increase
k	knit
k2tog	knit 2 stitches together
m	meters
mm	millimetres
oz	ounce
p	purl
p2tog	purl 2 stitches together
psso	pass the slipped stitch over
rev st st	reverse stockinette (stocking) stitch
sl	slip
ssk	slip slip knit
st(s)	stitch(es)
yd	yard

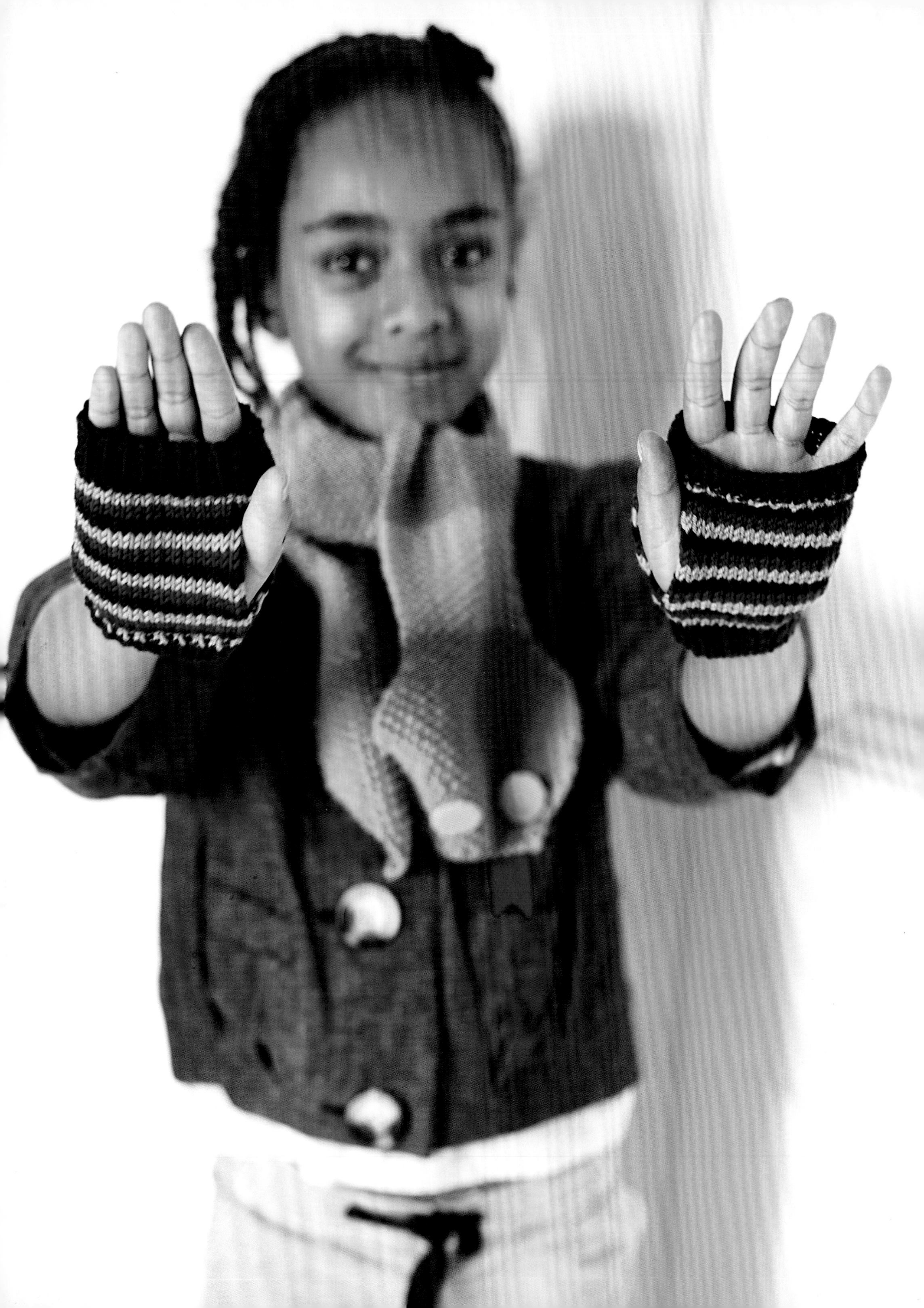

-Chapter 1
Cozy Knits

Cowl 22

Earmuffs 24

Little bear hat 28

Fingerless mitts 32

Rainbow earflap hat 34

Animal scarves 36

Panda hat 38

Pompom scarf 42

Octopus hat 44

Mouse mittens 48

Monster hat 51

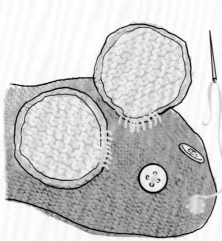

Cowl

A cowl is a bit like a scarf but it's not so long and the ends are joined together so they don't flap around. And, because it's shorter, it's even quicker and easier to knit than a scarf! This is made with very thick wool so it's quick to make and really snuggly and warm.

You will need

1 x 3½oz (100g) ball—approx 98yd (90m)—Rico Yarns Fashion Super Chunky (60% new wool, 40% acrylic), in shade 13 teal

Pair of US 13 (9mm) knitting needles

Darning needle

Finished size

One size, approx 18in (46cm) all around and 7¼in (18cm) wide

Techniques (see pages 9–19)

Garter stitch page 12

Sewing up page 15

Tip

You could make this in any yarn you have—it will just come out thinner or thicker depending on the thickness of the yarn. Choose a color to match or contrast with your coat.

1 Knit the cowl

Using US 13 (9mm) needles, cast on 20 stitches and keep knitting in garter stitch (every row knit stitch) until the piece is about 18in (46cm) long, or a length that you choose. Bind (cast) off all stitches.

2 Finish the cowl

Sew the two short sides together to form a tube, using a darning needle and matching yarn. You can wear it either as it is, or folded over to form a collar.

Earmuffs

If you don't like hats but can't stand having cold ears, earmuffs are for you—and they are great for when your friends just talk too loudly!

You will need

1 x 1¾oz (50g) ball—approx 98yd (90m)—of Patons Fairytale Dreamtime DK (100% pure wool), in each of:

Yarn A: shade 4953 pink
Yarn B: shade 4954 lilac
Yarn C: shade 4957 turquoise
Yarn D: shade 4952 lime
Yarn E: shade 4960 yellow

Pair of US 6 (4mm) knitting needles

Darning needle

Toy stuffing

Finished size

One size, approx 18in (46cm) from bottom of one ear to bottom of other

Abbreviations (see also page 19)

K2tog knit 2 stitches together

Techniques (see pages 9–19)

Decreasing page 13
Changing color page 14
Sewing up page 15
Finger knitting page 16

1 Knit the earmuff

Using US 6 (4mm) needles and yarn A, cast on 63 sts.
Row 1: Purl.
Change to yarn B.
Row 2: [K7, k2tog] to end of row. (56 sts)
Row 3: Purl.
Row 4: [K6, k2tog] to end of row. (49 sts)
Row 5: Purl.
Change to yarn C.
Row 6: [K5, k2tog] to end of row. (42 sts)
Row 7: Purl.
Row 8: [K4, k2tog] to end of row. (35 sts)
Row 9: Purl.
Change to yarn D.
Row 10: [K3, k2tog] to end of row. (28 sts)

Row 11: Purl.
Row 12: [K2, k2tog] to end of row. (21 sts)
Row 13: Purl.
Change to yarn E.
Row 14: [K1, k2tog] to end of row. (14 sts)
Row 15: Purl.
Row 16: [K2tog] to end of row. (7 sts)
Don't bind (cast) off.

Tip

You could use any DK or sportweight yarn but make sure it's warm and soft.

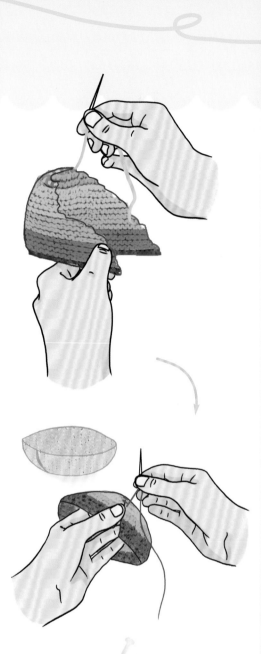

2 Make the earpieces
Thread the tail of the yellow yarn onto a darning needle and then thread it through the remaining yellow stitches and pull it up to form a tight circle. Sew up the side seam with overstitching.

Make the other stripy earmuff in the same way, then make two more in yarn E (yellow) for the backs.

Keep your ears TOASTY warm!

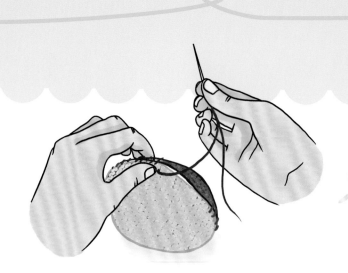

3 Sew the earpieces together

With both right sides facing outward, sew one striped circle to one plain circle. Sew almost all the way around the edge until there is just a small gap left. Leave your needle threaded.

4 Stuff the earpieces

Push small pieces of toy stuffing into the earmuff until it is firm and round and then sew up the gap. Do the same with the other two pieces.

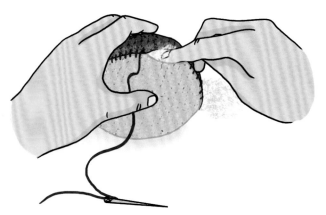

5 Knit the band

Using US 6 (4mm) needles and yarn A (pink), cast on 12 stitches and work in garter stitch for two rows. Change to lilac for another two rows and continue with two rows each of turquoise, lime, and yellow. Then go back to pink and continue like this with two rows of each color until the band measures 10in (25cm) long. Bind (cast) off.

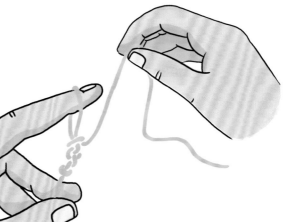

6

Finger knit the ties

Finger knit two lengths of chain approximately 19¾in (50cm) long.

7

Finish the earmuffs

Sew an earpiece to either end of the band, with all right sides facing out. (Check it fits before you sew!) Attach a tie to the bottom of each earmuff to fasten under your chin with a bow.

Little bear hat

This cute bear hat is knitted in an ultra-soft yarn on big needles, and the eyes and nose are made from felt, which means it is really quick to make. The details use embroidery stitches but you can change these to simple stitches if you prefer. It would make a great gift for a younger brother or sister.

You will need

2 x 1¾oz (50g) balls—approx 150yd (160m)—Wendy Norse Chunky (50% wool, 50% acrylic) in shade 2702 color eider (A)

Small amount of Sirdar Country Style DK (40% nylon, 30% wool, 30% acrylic) in shade 417 black (B)

Pair each of US 9 (5.5mm) and US 10½ (6.5mm) knitting needles

Darning needle

Large-eyed embroidery needle

Templates on page 124

Small amounts of black and cream felt

Sewing needle, cream and black sewing threads

Gauge (Tension)

14 sts and 20 rows to 4in (10 cm) square over stockinette (stocking) stitch using US 10.5 (6.5mm) needles.

Finished size

M(L): 5–10 years (11 years and over)

Approx 18½in (47cm) (20in[51cm]) circumference

Measure round your head to find the right size to knit

Abbreviations (see also page 19)

Inc increase
Knitwise insert the needle from left to right through the front of the stitch
Sl1 slip one stitch
Ssk slip, slip, knit
K2tog knit two stitches together
Psso pass slipped stitch over
P2tog purl two stitches together
Purlwise insert needle from right to left through the front of the stitch
RS right side
St st stockinette (stocking) stitch (one row knit, one row purl)
WS wrong side

Techniques (see pages 9–19)

Decreasing page 13

Increasing page 13

Flat seams page 15

Sewing up page 15

Embroidery stitches page 17–18

1 Knit the hat

Using US 9 (5.5mm) needles and yarn A, cast on 66(72) sts.
Knit 4 rows.
Change to US 10½ (6.5mm) needles.
Work 22(28) rows in st st beginning with a knit row.

Large size only:
Row 33: K5, [k2tog, k10] 3 times, [ssk, k10] twice, ssk, k5. (66 sts)
Row 34: Purl.
Both sizes:
Next row: [Sl1, k2tog, psso, k8] 5 times, sl1, k2tog, psso, k4. (54 sts)

Next and every WS row: Purl.
Next RS row: K3, [sl1, k2tog, psso, k6] 5 times, sl1, k2tog, psso, k3. (42 sts)
Next RS row: K2, [sl1, k2tog, psso, k4] 5 times, sl1, k2tog, psso, k2. (30 sts)
Next RS row: K1, [sl1, k2tog, psso, k2] 5 times, sl1, k2tog, psso, k1. (18 sts)
Next RS row: [Sl1, k2tog, psso] 6 times. (6 sts)
Break yarn leaving a long tail.
Thread the tail of yarn onto a darning needle and thread it through the remaining stitches, pull up tightly, and secure.

2 Knit the ears (make 2)
Using US 10½ (6.5mm) needles and yarn A, cast on 8 sts.
Work 5 rows in st st beginning with a knit row.
Row 6: P2tog, p4, p2tog. (6 sts)
Row 7: K2tog, k2, ssk. (4 sts)
Row 8: [P2tog] twice. (2 sts)
Row 9: [Inc1] twice. (4 sts)
Row 10: [Inc1 purlwise, p1] twice. (6 sts)
Row 11: Inc1, k3, inc1, k1. (8 sts)
Work 4 rows in st st beginning with a purl row.
Bind (cast) off knitwise on wrong side of work.

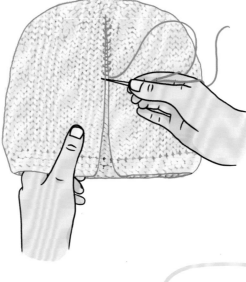

3

Sew the seam
Join the back seam of the hat together using the flat-seam technique.

4 Sew the ears

Fold the ear pieces in half widthwise, across the narrower section, with right sides together so the cast-on and bound- (cast-) off edges meet. Oversew around the curved edges then turn the ears right sides out and oversew the lower edges. Stitch the ears in place, stretching them very slightly so that they sit flat.

5 Cut out the felt pieces

Using the templates on page 124, draw and cut out a muzzle in cream felt and two eyes and a nose in black felt.

6 Sew the eyes
Using the black yarn (B) and a large-eyed needle, stitch the eyes in place using small running stitches. Make sure that you position them centrally on the front of the hat.

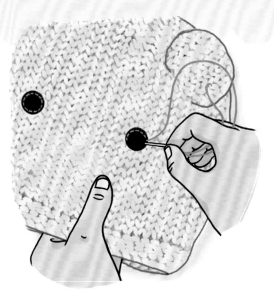

7 Sew the muzzle
Using cream thread and a sewing needle, work a row of small running stitches around the muzzle, close to the edge, to stitch it in place on the hat. Then oversew the nose on the muzzle using black thread and a sewing needle.

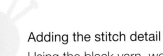

8 Adding the stitch detail
Using the black yarn, work a row of chain stitch from the nose to the bottom of the muzzle (or use a couple of long straight stitches if you find them easier).

Fingerless mitts

There are times when your hands and wrists are cold but gloves are no use because they mean you can't use your fingers properly. That's when you need fingerless mittens. They are really easy to make as they are just rectangles sewn up the side and they are bright and stylish too. Knit them as long or short as you wish, depending on how warm you want your arms to be.

You will need

1 x 1¾oz (50g) ball—approx 131yd (120m)—Rico Essentials Merino DK (100% merino wool), in each of:

Yarn A: shade 38 dark blue
Yarn B: shade 23 light blue
Yarn C: shade 18 bright blue

Pair each of US 5 (3.75mm) and US 6 (4mm) knitting needles

Darning needle

Finished size

Measure just above your wrist to see which size you need. The wrist widths are:

Small: approx 6¾ in (17cm)

Medium: approx 7½ in (19cm)

Large: approx 8¼ in (21cm)

The pattern gives two different lengths but you can make your mitts whatever length you want.

Abbreviations (see page 19)

Techniques (see pages 9–19)

Changing color page 14

Sewing up page 15

---

1 Knit the mitts
Using US 5 (3.75mm) needles and yarn A, cast on:

37 stitches for the small size
41 stitches for the medium size
45 stitches for the large size.
Row 1: K1, [p1, k1] to end of row.
Row 2: P1, [k1, p1] to end of row.
This is rib stitch. Repeat these same two rows until your work is 1in (2.5cm) for short mitts, or 4¼in (11cm) for long mitts (or as long as you want them). End with a row 2.
Change to US 6 (4mm) needles and yarn B.
Row 1: Knit.
Row 2: Purl.
Change to yarn C.
Row 3: Knit.
Row 4: Purl.
Change to yarn A.
Row 5: Knit.
Row 6: Purl.
Continue in stockinette (stocking) stitch (one row knit, one row purl) as for rows 1–6, changing color every two rows until the stripy part measures 2½in (6cm) for small, 2¾in (7cm) for medium, or 3¼in (8cm) for

Tip

The small size will fit most children's wrists—knit the larger sizes for older siblings or as a gift for your mom!

large. End with a purl row.
Change to US 5 (3.75mm) needles and yarn A.
Row 1: K1, [p1, k1] to end of row.
Row 2: P1, [k1, p1] to end of row.
Repeat these two rows once more.
Bind (cast) off all stitches.

2 Sew up the mitts
For both lengths, sew up the side seam on each glove from the bottom of the long rib to ½in (1cm) above the beginning of the striped section.

3 Leave a gap of 1½in (4cm) for your thumb and then sew up the rest of the seam to the end.

Warm WRISTS—FREE fingers!

Rainbow earflap hat

A rainbow striped hat to cheer you up and keep you warm on cold and dreary days. This yarn changes color as you knit, so you get a stripy hat without having to keep changing yarns—easy!

You will need

2(2) x 1¾oz (50g) balls—each approx 95yd (87m)—Crystal Palace Yarns, Mochi Plus (80% merino wool, 20% nylon), in shade 551 intense rainbow

Pair of US 8 (5mm) knitting needles

2 stitch holders

Darning needle

Gauge (Tension)

18 sts and 24 rows to 4in (10cm) in stockinette (stocking) stitch using US 8 (5mm) needles.

Finished size

Medium: age 3-10 years; head circumference 17in (43cm)

Large: age 11years and over; head circumference 20in/51cm

Measure around your head to find out which size to knit.

Abbreviations (see also page 19)

Inc increase
K2tog knit 2 stitches together
WS wrong side
St st stockinette (stocking) stitch
  (one row knit, one row purl)

Techniques (see pages 9–19)

Increasing page 13

Decreasing page 13

Picking up stitches page 14

Sewing up page 15

1 Knit the earflaps (make two)
Using US 8 (5mm) needles, cast on 6 sts.
Row 1 (WS): Purl.
Row 2: Inc1, k to last st, inc1.
Repeat last two rows until there are 18 sts.
Next row: Purl.
Leave each earflap on a stitch holder.

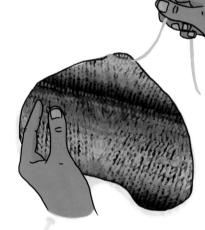

2 Knit the hat
First join in the earflaps.
Using US 8 (5mm) needles, cast on 12(14) sts,
Slide the 18 sts from first earflap onto your left needle with the right side facing you.
Knit across these stitches.
Now cast on 32(36) more stitches.
Slide the 18 sts from the second earflap onto your left needle with the right side facing you.
Knit these stitches.
Cast on 12(14) stitches. (92(100) sts)
Row 1 (WS): Purl across all sts.
Row 2: Knit.
Continue in st st in this way on these 92(100) sts until work measures 4¾in [12cm] (5½in [14cm]) from cast-on brim, ending with a purl row.

Begin decreasing for the crown

Row 1: [K4, k2tog] to last 2(4) sts, k2(4).
(77(84) sts)

Beginning with a p row, work 3 rows st st.

Row 5: [K3, k2tog] to last 2(4) sts, k2(4).
(62(68) sts)

Beginning with a p row, work 3 rows st st.

Row 9: [K2, k2tog] to last 2(4) sts, k2(4).
(47(52) sts)

Row 10 (and every other row): Purl.

Row 11: [K1, k2tog] to last 2(4) sts, k2(4).
(32(36) sts

Row 13: [K2tog] to end of row. (16(18) sts)

Work in st st on these sts for 1¼in (3cm).

K2tog to end of row. (8(9) sts)

Thread the long tail of yarn onto a darning needle and then thread the yarn through the remaining stitches, pull up tight.

KNIT a rainbow!

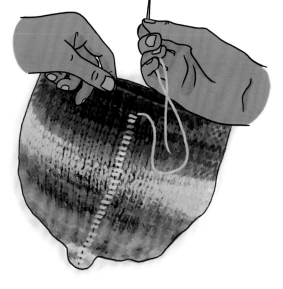

Finish the hat

Rejoin the yarn to one end of the lower edge.

With right side facing, pick up and knit 107[115] sts all along the edge.

Row 1 (WS): [K1, p1] to last st, k1.

Row 2: [P1, k1] to last st, p1.

Repeat rows 1–2 once more.

Bind (cast) off loosely in rib. Sew up the side seam.

Animal scarves

Use the basic scarf pattern with a head at one end and a tail at the other to create your own animal, using felt, buttons, and fabric. This scarf uses seed (moss) stitch which is a bit tricky, so only attempt it when you are becoming more confident at your knitting.

You will need

....

1¾oz (50g)—each approx 98yd (90m)—Debbie Bliss Cashmerino Aran (55% merino wool, 33% microfiber, 12% cashmere), in:

Snake
Yarn A: 2 x balls shade 502 lime
Yarn B: 1 x ball shade 034 yellow

Cat
Yarn A: 2 x balls shade 003 orange
Yarn B: 1 x ball shade 009 gray

Pair of US 7 (4.5mm) knitting needles

Buttons for eyes

Templates on page 124

Felt for tongue and ears or other features

Darning needle

Sewing needle and thread

Finished size

The scarf is about 5in (12.5cm) wide and you can make it as long as you like.

Abbreviations (see also page 19)

Inc increase

Techniques (see pages 9–19)

Increasing page 13

Changing colors page 14

Sewing buttons page 17

Embroidery stitches page 17–18

---

1 **Knit the scarf**
Using US 7 (4.5mm) needles and yarn A, cast on 3 sts.
Row 1: K1, p1, k1.
Row 2: Inc1, p1, inc1. (5 sts)
Row 3: P1, [k1, p1] to end of row.
Row 4: Inc1, k1, p1, k1, inc1. (7 sts)
Row 5: K1, [p1, k1] to end of row. This makes a pattern called seed (moss) stitch.
Row 6: Inc1, p1, work seed (moss) st to last st, inc1. (9 sts)
Row 7: P1, [k1, p1] to end of row.
Row 8: Inc1, k1, work seed (moss) st to last st, inc1. (11 sts)

Row 9: K1, [p1, k1] to end of row.
Row 10: Inc1, p1, work seed (moss) st to last st, inc1. (13 sts)
Row 11: P1, [k1, p1] to end of row.
Row 12: Inc1, k1, work seed (moss) st to last st, inc1. (15 sts)
Row 13: K1, [p1, k1] to end of row.
Row 14: Inc1, p1, work seed (moss) st to last st, inc1. (17 sts)
Row 15: P1, [k1, p1] to end of row.
Row 16: Inc1, k1, work seed (moss) st to last st, inc1. (19 sts)
Row 17: K1, [p1, k1] to end of row.
Row 18: Inc1, p1, work seed (moss) st to last st, inc1. (21 sts)
Row 19: P1, [k1, p1] to end of row.
Row 20: Inc1, k1, work seed (moss) st to last st, inc1. (23 sts)

Row 21: K1, [p1, k1] to end of row. Repeat row 21 for 2¼in (6cm).

Change to yarn B and work 2¼in (6cm) as row 21.
Change to yarn A and work 2¼in (6cm) as row 21.
Continue working as row 21, changing color every 2¼in (6cm) until scarf measures approx 1yd (1m), ending with a yarn B stripe.
Change to yarn A and work 4 rows in pattern.

Shape head
Row 1: Increase one stitch at either end of row, keeping to seed (moss)

stitch in the same pattern as before.

Row 2: Work straight in seed (moss) stitch.
Repeat last two rows until you have 31 sts.
Work straight in seed (moss) stitch pattern for 15 rows.

Next row: K2tog, work in seed (moss) stitch to last two sts, k2tog. (29 sts)

Next row: Work straight in seed (moss) stitch.
Repeat last two rows until you have 17 sts.
Bind (cast) off all stitches.

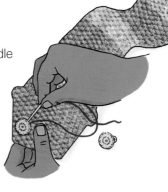

2

Add the eyes
Using a darning needle and yarn, attach the buttons to the head for eyes, positioning them about 2in (5cm) up from the end of the scarf.

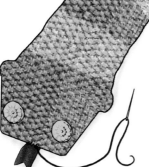

3

Finishing a snake scarf
For the snake, use the template on page 124 to draw and cut a forked tongue in red felt. Sew it to the bottom of the head on the wrong side. Use small overstitches to make sure it is securely attached.

4

Finishing a cat scarf
If you have knitted a cat scarf, sew on eyes in the same way as for the snake.
Use the templates on page 124 to draw and cut two ears in gray felt and one tongue in pink felt. Sew these to the head using over stitches. Use a darning needle and yarn to stitch on a triangular nose with a few straight stitches, and add the mouth with backstitch. You could add some whiskers too.

Panda hat

Who can resist the cuteness of a panda? We all love them and we all care for them. Remind everyone of how wonderful these animals are with this striking hat.

You will need

1 x 1¾oz (50g) ball—approx 127yd (116m)—Sublime Extra Fine Merino DK (100% extra fine merino wool), in shade 13 jet black (A)

1(2) x 1¾oz (50g) ball(s)—each approx 98yds (90m)—Patons Fairytale DK in shade 51 white (B)

Pair each US 9 (5.5mm) and US 3 (3.25mm) knitting needles

Darning needle

Large embroidery needle

Gauge (Tension)

16 sts and 21 rows to 4in (10cm) square over stockinette (stocking) stitch using yarn DOUBLE on US 9 (5.5mm) needles.

Finished size

Small: age 3–10 years; head circumference 17in (43cm)

Medium: age 11years and over; head circumference 20in/51cm

Measure around your head to find out which size to knit.

NOTE Remember if you are knitting the medium size you follow the instruction in round brackets, which come second. For example, *Cast on 66 (78) stitches*, means for the small size cast on 66 stitches, for the medium size, cast on 78 stitches.

Abbreviations (see page 19)

SL slip a stitch
K2tog knit two stitches together
Psso pass slipped stitch over
P2tog purl 2 stitches together
Ssk slip slip knit
Purlwise

Techniques (see pages 9–19)

Decreasing page 13

Increasing page 13

Flat seam page 15

Embroidery stitches pages 17–18

1 Knit the hat

Using US 9 (5.5mm) needles and yarn A, cast on 66(78) stitches using yarn double (two strands held together).

Row 1: [K2, p2] to last 2 sts, k2.
Row 2: [P2, k2] to last 2 sts, p2.
Repeat rows 1–2 once more.
Break yarn A and join in yarn B, again using yarn double.
Work 24(28) rows in st st beginning with a knit row.
Medium size only:
Row 33: K5, [sl1, k2tog, psso, k10] 5 times, sl1, k2tog, psso, k5. (66 sts)
Row 34: Purl.
Both sizes:
Next row: K4, [sl1, k2tog, psso, k8] 5 times, sl1, k2tog, psso, k4. (54 sts)
Next and every WS row until stated otherwise: Purl.
Next RS row: K3, [sl1, k2tog, psso, k6] 5 times, sl1, k2tog, psso, k3. (42 sts)
Next RS row: K2, [sl1, k2tog, psso, k4] 5 times, sl1, k2tog, psso, k2. (30 sts)
Next RS row: K1, [sl1, k2tog, psso, k2] 5 times, sl1, k2tog, psso, k1. (18 sts)
Next row (WS): [P2tog] to end. (9 sts)
Break yarn leaving a long tail.
Thread yarn tail through remaining sts, pull up tightly and secure.

Save the PANDA!

2 Knit the ears (make 2)
Using US 9 (5.5mm) needles and yarn A, cast on 10 sts using yarn double.
Work 6 rows in st st beginning with a knit row.
Row 7: K2tog, k6, ssk. (8 sts)
Row 8: P2tog, p4, p2tog. (6 sts)
Row 9: K2tog, k2, ssk. (4 sts)
Row 10: [P2tog] twice. (2 sts)
Row 11: [Inc1] twice. (4 sts)
Row 12: [Inc1 purlwise, p1] twice. (6 sts)
Row 13: Inc1, k3, inc1, k1. (8 sts)
Row 14: Inc1 purlwise, p5, inc1 purlwise, p1. (10 sts)
Work 6 rows in st st beginning with a knit row.
Bind (cast) off.

3 Knit the eye patches (make 2)
Using US 3 (3.25mm) needles and yarn A, cast on 6 sts.
Row 1: Inc1, k to last 2 sts, inc1, k1. (8 sts)
Row 2: Inc1 purlwise, p to last 2 sts, inc1 purlwise, p1. (10 sts)
Repeat rows 1–2 once more. (14 sts)
Work 6 rows in st st beginnig with a knit row.
Row 11: K2tog, k to last 2 sts, ssk. (12 sts)
Row 12: P2tog, p to last 2 sts, p2tog. (10 sts)
Repeat rows 11–12 once more. (6 sts)
Bind (cast) off.

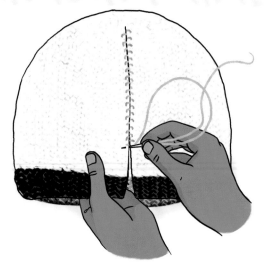

4 Sew the seam
Join the back seam of the hat together using the flat-seam technique (see page 15).

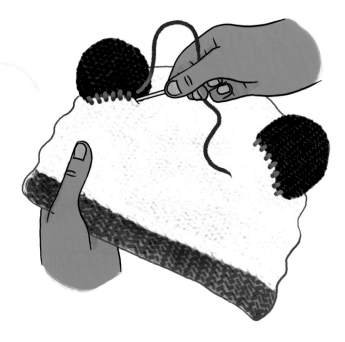

5 Sew the ears
Fold the ear pieces in half widthwise with right sides together so the top and bottom edges meet. Oversew around the curved edges then turn the ears right side out. Oversew the lower edges. Stitch the ears in place, stretching them very slightly so that they sit flat.

Tip

Instead of knitting the eyes and using embroidery for the nose and mouth, you could cut them out of felt and sew them on.

6 Sew the eye patches

Oversew the eye patches in place so they slope slightly downward toward the sides of hat.

7 Embroider the eye

Using white yarn (B), embroider a coil of chain stitch for each eye, leaving a gap in the center of the eyes for the pupil.

8 Embroider the mouth

Using black yarn (A), embroider a coil of chain stitch in a triangle shape for the nose and work a row of chain stitch from the nose to the top of the ribbed border of the hat.

Pompom scarf

A plain scarf is one of the easiest things to knit but it's not very exciting. Make this one fun and different by attaching a whole ball pool of brightly colored pompoms!

You will need

1 x 1¾oz (50g) ball—approx 98yd (90m) of Aran weight wool for the scarf, such as Debbie Bliss Cashmerino Aran (55% wool, 33% acrylic, 12% cashmere), in shade 502 lime

Leftover oddments of yarn in different colors to make the pompoms

Pair of US 9 (5.5mm) needles

Cardstock or pompom maker in assorted sizes

Finished size

You can knit the scarf to any length that you choose

Techniques (see pages 9–19)

Garter stitch page 12

Making pompoms page 16

1 Knit the scarf
Using US 9 (5.5mm) needles and the main scarf yarn, cast on 15 stitches. Work in garter stitch (every row knit) until the scarf is a length you like. Bind (cast) off.

2 Make the pompoms
Using cardstock rings or a pompom maker, make at least 12 pompoms in assorted colors and sizes. Thread a darning needle with a long piece of yarn and secure it to one corner of the scarf with a few stitches over and over in the same place. Now thread the yarn through 3 different sized pompoms, all in different colors and then thread it back the other way. Secure it back to the same corner of the scarf with a few more stitches.
In the same way attach three or four more pompoms to each corner of the scarf.

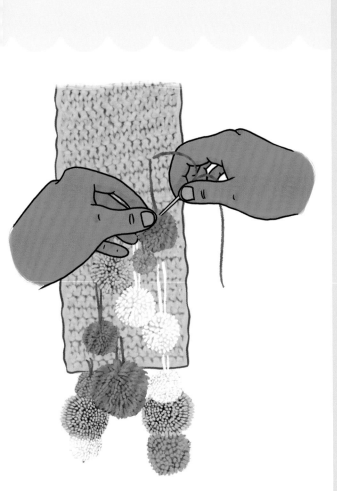

3 You can attach single pompoms along the scarf, too. Simply leave a long tail when tying off the pompom, thread it onto a darning needle, and attach it through a stitch on the scarf. Secure the thread in the center of the pompom with a few stitches.

Pompom FUN

Octopus hat

Cute and colorful—the tentacles of this octopus hat will really get you noticed! The tentacles are made using crochet but you could always make them by braiding (plaiting) thick bunches of wool instead.

You will need

2 x 1¾oz (50g) balls—approx 340yds (310m)—Sirdar Country Style DK (40% nylon, 30% wool, 30% acrylic), in shade 527 rosehip (A)

Small amount black (B) and white (C) DK yarn for the embroidery

Pair of US 9 (5.5mm) knitting needles

Stitch marker

US J-10 (6mm) crochet hook

Darning needle

Gauge (Tension)

16 sts and 22 rows to 4in (10cm) square over stockinette (stocking) stitch using yarn DOUBLE on US 9 (5.5 mm) needles.

Finished size

Small: age 3–10 years; head circumference 17in (43cm)

Medium: age 11years and over; head circumference 20in (51cm)

Measure around your head to find out which size to knit.

NOTE Remember if you are knitting the medium size you follow the instruction in round brackets, which come second. For example, Cast on 66(78) stitches, means for the small size cast on 66 stitches, for the medium size, cast on 78 stitches.

Abbreviations (see also page 19)

K2tog1 knit 2 stitches together
Psso pass slipped stitch over
P2tog purl 2 stitches together
Ssk slip slip knit
WS wrong side

Techniques (see pages 9–19)

Decreasing page 13

Picking up stitches page 14

Flat seams page 15

Embroidery stitches pages 17–19

---

1 Knit the hat

Using US 9 (5.5mm) needles and yarn A double (two strands held together), cast on 66(78) sts.
Place a small safety pin marker on 23rd(26th) stitch in from each edge.
Knit 4 rows.
Work 22(26) rows in st st beginning with a knit row.
Medium size only:
Row 31: K5, [sl1, k2tog, psso, k10] 5 times, sl1, k2tog, psso, k5. (66 sts)
Row 32: Purl.

Both sizes:
Next row: K4, [sl1, k2tog, psso, k8] 5 times, sl1, k2tog, psso, k4. (54 sts)
Next and every WS row until stated otherwise: Purl.
Next RS row: K3, [sl1, k2tog, psso, k6] 5 times, sl1, k2tog, psso, k3. (42 sts)
Next RS row: K2, [sl1, k2tog, psso, k4] 5 times, sl1, k2tog, psso, k2. (30 sts)
Next RS row: K1, [sl1, k2tog, psso, k2] 5 times, sl1, k2tog, psso, k1. (18 sts)
Next row (WS): [P2tog] to end. (9 sts)
Break yarn leaving a long tail.

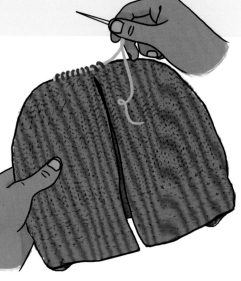

Thread yarn tail through remaining sts, pull up tightly, and secure.

Toss those TENTACLES!

With RS of work facing and using yarn A double, pick up and knit 23(26) sts across lower edge from RH edge toward first safety pin marker.
Next row: Knit.
Next row: Knit to last 2 sts, k2tog. (22(25) sts)
Repeat last 2 rows twice (3 times) more. (20(22) sts)
Bind (cast) off.

With RS of work facing and using a doubled strand of yarn A, pick up and knit 23(26) sts across lower edge from second safety pin marker to LH edge.
Next row: Knit.
Next row: Ssk, knit to end. (22(25) sts)
Rep last 2 rows 2(3) times more. (20(22) sts)
Bind (cast) off.

2 Crochet the tentacles

Measure and cut 8 lengths of pink yarn (A), each measuring 8½yd (7.5m). Fold each length in half, then in half again twice more; each length will now consist of eight strands of yarn.

Using the crochet hook, work eight 6¼in (16 cm) crochet chains. Do this by making a slip knot on the crochet hook, like you would to start your knitting. Holding the slip stitch on the hook, wind the yarn around the hook from the back to the front, then catch the yarn in the crochet-hook tip. Pull the yarn through the slip stitch on your crochet hook to make the second link in the chain. Keep going until your chain is the right length. Trim the ends of the yarn to 1in (2.5cm) long.

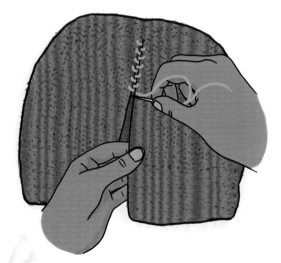

3 Sew the seam

Join the back seam of the hat together using the flat-seam technique.

4 Add the eyes

Using a doubled strand of black yarn (B), work two French knots for eyes. Using white yarn (C), embroider three circles of chain stitch around each French knot.

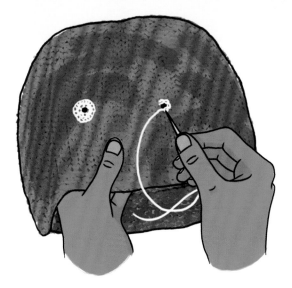

5 Sew the mouth

Using black yarn (B), work a 2½in (6cm) row of chain stitch for the mouth, just above the edge of the hat and between the eyes.

6 Add the tentacles

Sew one tentacle at each side of the lower edge of the hat, sewing in place with small overstitches. Space the other tentacles evenly between them.

Mouse mittens

These sweet little mittens will keep you warm and act as a toy at the same time! You could put on your own puppet show and make each hand a different animal!

You will need

1(1) x 1¾oz (50g) ball—each approx 131yd (120m)—Artesano Inca Cloud (100% alpaca), in each of:

Yarn A: shade ZK gray

Yarn B: shade B432 pink

Pair each of US 3 (3.25mm) and US 5 (3.75mm) knitting needles

Darning needle

Buttons for eyes

Finished size

S(M): age 6–8 (9–11) yrs

Gauge (Tension)

24 sts and 32 rows to 4in (10cm) in stockinette (stocking) stitch using US 5 (3.75mm) needles.

Abbreviations (see also page 19)

dec decrease
inc increase
k2tog knit 2 stitches together
RS right side
st st stockinette (stocking) stitch (one row knit, one row purl)

Techniques (see pages 9–19)

Increasing page 13

Sewing buttons page 17

Sewing up page 15

Embroidery stitches pages 17–18

1 **Knit the mittens**
Using US 3 (3.25mm) needles and yarn A, cast on 41(45) sts.
Row 1(RS): K2, [p1, k1] to last st, k1.
Row 2: P2, [k1, p1] to last st, p1.
Repeat these two rows until rib measures 1½in (4cm), ending with a row 2.
Change to larger needles and st st and work 6(8) rows st st, beginning with a knit row.
Increase for Thumb:
Row 1: K19(21), inc into next st, k1, inc into next st, knit to end. (43(47) sts)
Row 2 (and every even row): Purl.
Row 3: K19(21), inc into next st, k3, inc into next st, knit to end. (45(49) sts)

Row 5: K19(21), inc into next st, k5, inc into next st, knit to end. (47(51) sts)
Continue to inc for thumb gusset in this way until you have 49(55) sts, ending with a knit row.
Next row: Purl.
Next row: K30(34), cast on 1 st, turn, leaving remaining sts unworked.
Next row: P12(14), cast on 1 st, turn and continue to work just on these 13(15) sts for 1½in (4cm), ending with a purl row.
Shape Thumb Top:
Next row: [K1, k2tog] to last 1(0) st, k1(0). (9(10) sts)
Next row: Purl.
Next row: K1(0), [k2tog] to end. (5 sts)
Break off yarn and thread through remaining sts, pull up tightly and secure, sew up thumb seam.

Hand
With RS facing, rejoin yarn, pick up and knit 3 sts along base of thumb, knit remaining 19(21) unworked sts on left-hand needle.
Purl across all sts. (41(45) sts)
Work in st st for 2(2¼)in (5(6)cm) ending with a purl row.
Shape Top:
Row 1: [K1, k2tog, k15(17), k2tog] twice, k1. (37(41) sts)
Row 2 (and every even row): Purl.
Row 3: [K1, k2tog, k13(15), k2tog] twice, k1. (33(37) sts)
Row 5: [K1, k2tog, k11(13), k2tog] twice, k1. (29(33) sts)
Row 7: [K1, k2tog, k9(11), k2tog] twice, k1. (25(29) sts)

Continue dec 4 sts every row as established until you have 17 sts.
Break off yarn and thread through remaining sts, pull up tightly and secure, sew up side seam.

Outer Ears
Using US 5 (3.75mm) needles and yarn A, cast on 5 sts.
Row 1: Knit.
Row 2: Purl.
Row 3: Inc1, knit to last st, inc1. (7 sts)
Row 4: Purl.
Row 5: Inc1, knit to last st, inc1. (9 sts)
Work three rows st st.
Row 9: K2tog, knit to last 2 sts, k2tog. (7 sts)
Row 10: Purl.
Row 11: K2tog, knit to last 2 sts, k2tog. (5 sts)
Row 12: Purl.
Bind (cast) off all sts.
Make three more pieces the same.

Inner Ears
Using US 5 (3.75mm) needles and yarn B, cast on 5 sts.
Rows 1–2: Knit.
Row 3: Inc1, knit to last st, inc1. (7 sts)
Row 4: Knit.
Row 5: Inc1, knit to last st, inc1. (9 sts)
Work four rows garter st (knit every row).
Row 10: Ktog, knit to last 2 sts, k2tog. (7 sts)
Row 11: Knit.
Row 12: Ktog, knit to last 2 sts, k2tog. (5 sts)
Row 13: Knit.
Bind (cast) off all sts.
Make three more pieces the same.

2

Make the ears
Using a darning needle and matching yarn, sew one gray stocking stitch circle to one pink garter stitch circle to make an ear. Make sure that you place the right side of the grey outer ear on the outside. Make up all four ears like this.

3
Using a darning needle and matching yarn, sew two ears to the top side of each mitten.

4 Add the eyes and nose
To each mitten, attach two small buttons for eyes. At the tip of the mitten embroider a nose in pink yarn (B) using three or four straight stitches. You could add some twitching whiskers too!

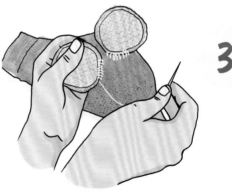

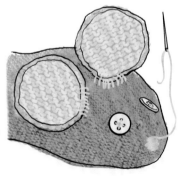

Squeak SQUEAK squeak!

Monster hat

If you have some oddments of chunky yarn this is the perfect hat for you to knit—monsters can come in any color and who says the horns need to be the same color as the head or that eyes should be pink and the mouth green?! Just go wild with your color scheme and enjoy making something fun and different.

You will need

1(2) x 1¾oz (50g) ball(s)—each approx 49yd (45m)—Sirdar Big Softie (51% wool, 49% acrylic) in shade 343 bling blue (A)

Small amount of DK black yarn (B)

Pair of US 10.5 (6.5mm) knitting needles

Darning needle

Round object to draw around, like a bobbin or button, with a diameter of about 1in (2.5cm)

Small pieces of colored felt

7/8in (22mm) button

Sewing needle and sewing threads

Gauge (Tension)

12 sts and 17 rows to 4in (10cm) square over stockinette (stocking) stitch using US 10.5 (6.5mm) needles.

Finished size

Small: age 3-10 years; head circumference 17in (43cm)

Medium: age 11years and over; head circumference 20in/51cm

Measure around your head to find out which size to knit.

Remember if you are knitting the medium size you follow the instruction in round brackets which come second. For example, *Cast on 54 (60) stitches*. That means for the small size cast on 54 stitches, for the medium size, cast on 60 stitches.

Abbreviations (see also page 19)

K2tog knit 2 stitches together
Ssk   slip slip knit
Psso   pass slipped stitch over

Techniques (see pages 9–19)

Decreasing page 13

Flat seams page 15

Embroidery stitches pages 17–18

Sewing buttons page 17

1 Knit the hat
Using US 10.5 (6.5mm) needles and yarn A, cast on 54(60) sts.
Knit 4 rows.
Work 16(18) rows in st st beginning with a knit row.
Medium size only:
Row 23: K4, [k2tog, k8] 3 times, [ssk, k8] twice, ssk, k4. (54 sts)
Row 24: Purl.

Both sizes:
Next row: K3, [sl1, k2tog, psso, k6] 5 times, sl1, k2tog, psso, k3. (42 sts)
Next and every WS row: Purl.
Next RS row: K2, [sl1, k2tog, psso, k4] 5 times, sl1, k2tog, psso, k2. (30 sts)
Next RS row: K1, [sl1, k2tog, psso, k2] 5 times, sl1, k2tog, psso, k1. (18 sts)
Next RS row: [Sl1, k2tog, psso] 6 times. (6 sts)

Break yarn leaving a long tail. Thread yarn tail through remaining sts, pull up tightly and secure.

2 Knit the horns (make 2)
Using US 10.5 (6.5mm) needles
and yarn A, cast on 4(6) sts.
Work 10 rows in st st beginning
with a knit row.
Bind (cast) off.

3 Sew the seam
Join the back seam of the hat together using
the flat-seam technique.

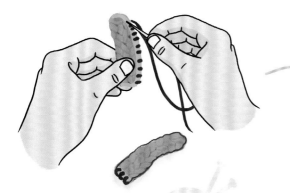

4 Sew the horns
Fold the horn pieces in half lengthwise so that the right
side is on the outside. Oversew the top and side seams
with matching yarn. Stitch the horns in place using small
oversewing stitches.

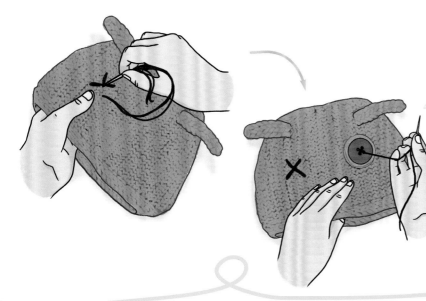

5 Add the eyes
Using black yarn (B), stitch a
large cross stitch for one eye.
Draw around the round object on
the felt and cut out a circle for the
other eye. Position this in place then
sew the button to the hat through the
center of the circle using black
sewing thread.

6

Add the nose

Cut a rectangle of a different color for the nose. Make it about 1in (2.5cm) long and ½in (1cm) wide (use a straight corner of your piece of felt and a ruler and pencil to help you draw the shape). Using the same color sewing thread, oversew the nose in place. Using black yarn (B), work two straight stitches, one over the other, from the bottom of the nose to the top of the garter-stitch hat border.

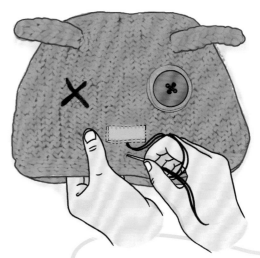

Chapter 2

Stylish Knits

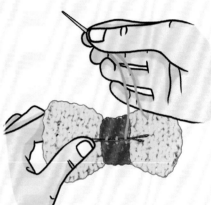

Little bows 56

Legwarmers 58

Decorative buttons 60

MP3 or phone cover 62

Pompom necklace 64

Ballet slippers 67

Tassel belt 70

Heart key ring charm 73

Pencil case 76

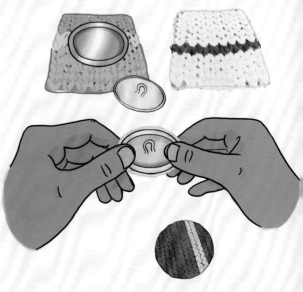

Little bows

Sweet bows to put in your hair or wear as brooches. Make them with any left-over yarns you have and mix and match the colors. You can make them bigger or smaller as you wish—just cast on more stitches for a wider bow and knit a longer length for a longer one.

You will need

....

Left over DK weight yarns in a variety of colors

Pair of US 6 (4mm) knitting needles

Darning needle

Safety pins, brooch backs, hair grips

Sewing needle and thread

Finished size

Approx 2¾in (7cm) wide

Techniques (see pages 9–19)

Garter stitch page 12

Stockinette (stocking) stitch page 12

Sewing up page 15

1 Knit the main bow
Using US 6 (4mm) knitting needles and any yarn, cast on 10 stitches and work in garter stitch (every row knit) for about 5½in (14cm), or twice as long as you want the bow to be. Bind (cast) off.
Using matching yarn, sew the short ends together to form a loop

2 Knit the center strip
Using US 6 (4mm) needles and a different color of yarn, cast on 5 stitches and work in stockinette (stocking) stitch (one row knit, one row purl) for 10 rows. Bind (cast) off.

3 Make the bow
Wrap the smaller strip around the middle of the loop. Sew the short ends together at the back.

MIX and match!

4 Finally, use a sewing needle and thread to sew a hairgrip, brooch back, or safety pin to the back of the bow. Sew small stitches over the hairgrip or pin right along its length. Start and finish off by sewing several stitches over and over in one place to secure the thread.

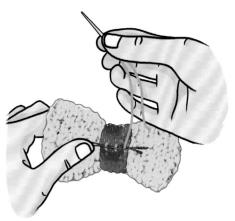

Legwarmers

These legwarmers are great for keeping you warm in winter or for wearing to dance or gym classes.

You will need

....

1 x 1¾oz (50g) ball—approx 98yd (90m)—Debbie Bliss Cashmerino Aran (55% merino wool, 33% microfiber, 12% cashmere), in each of:

Yarn A: shade 31 dark purple
Yarn B: shade 17 light purple

Pair each of US 7 (4.5mm) and US 8 (5mm) knitting needles

Darning needle

Finished size

Small: 8¼in (21cm)

Medium: 9in (23cm)

Large: 10in (25cm)

Measure your leg around your calf to see which size you need. You can make the leg warmers as long or as short as you wish.

Abbreviations (see page 19)

Techniques (see pages 9–19)

Rib stitch page 12

Stockinette (stocking) stitch page 12

Changing color page 14

Sewing up page 15

1 **Knit the legwarmers**
Using US 7 (4.5mm) needles and yarn A (dark purple) cast on:
37 stitches for the small size
41 stitches for the medium size
45 stitches for the large size.

Row 1: K1, [p1, k1] to end of row.
Row 2: P1, [k1, p1] to end of row.
This is rib stitch. Repeat these same two rows until your work is 4in (10cm) long. End with a row 2.
Change to US 8 (5mm) needles and yarn B (light purple).
Next row: Knit.
Next row: Purl.

This is stockinette (stocking) stitch. Continue like this—one row knit, one row purl—until the light purple section is 6in (15cm) long, or as long as you want it. End with a purl row.
Change back to US 7 (4.5mm) needles and yarn A (dark purple).
Next row: K1, [p1, k1] to end of row.
Next row: P1, [k1, p1] to end of row.
Repeat these last two rib rows for a further 4in (10cm).
Bind (cast) off all stitches.
Knit another leg warmer to match the first!

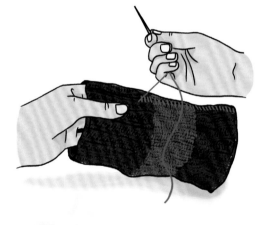

2 **Finish the legwarmers**
Sew up the long side seam of each legwarmer using overstitch.

Keep DANCING!

Decorative buttons

Use up all your scraps of yarn making these bright and beautiful covered buttons to liven up old clothes or to use as badges on coats and bags. They are so small you can knit them in minutes!

You will need

Oddments of yarn from all the DK/worsted weight projects in the book

Pair of US 6 (4mm) needles

Darning needle

Self-cover buttons kit

Finished size

Buttons used are: large 1½in (38mm); medium 1¼in (29mm); small ⅞in (23mm)

Techniques (see pages 9–19)

Stockinette (stocking) stitch page 12

Changing color page 14

Sewing buttons page 17

1 Knit the buttons
Using US 6 (4mm) needles and any yarn, cast on:
For large buttons: 11 stitches
For medium buttons: 8 stitches
For small buttons: 5 stitches.

Work in stockinette (stocking) stitch (one row knit, one row purl) until you have knitted a square. To test if it is square, fold the knitting from corner to corner—a square will fold perfectly in half. Add stripes wherever you want them! Bind (cast) off all stitches.

2 Finish the buttons
Put the knitted square on the table, right side facing down. Self-cover buttons come in two pieces with a front and a back (there will be instructions with the kit). Take the front of the button and put it in the middle of square. Fold the edges over to the back, where there are little teeth to catch the knitting and hold it firm. Make sure it is tucked in all the way round and then press on the back piece. (You may need an adult with strong fingers to help. Sew the buttons to your clothes, bags, pencil cases—whatever needs brightening up!

Bright as a **BUTTON!**

MP3 or phone cover

Knit this cover and you can keep your phone or MP3 player snug and warm—or at least safe from knocks and scratches! It's only small so you can use up any scraps of DK wool for this.

You will need

....

1 x 1¾oz (50g) ball—approx 137yd (125m)—Millamia Merino (100% merino wool), in each of:

Yarn A: shade 161 seaside
Yarn B: shade 120 forget-me-not

Pair of US 3 (3.25mm) knitting needles

Darning needle

Button, about ¾in (2cm) in diameter

Needle and thread

Finished size

This makes a case about 4¾in (12cm) long by 2in (5cm) wide but it will stretch to 2¾in (7cm) wide. Cast on more stitches for a wider cover.

Abbreviations (see page 19)

Techniques (see pages 9–19)

Changing color page 14

Sewing up page 15

Finger knitting page 16

Sewing buttons page 17

1 Knit the cover
Using US 3 (3.25mm) needles and yarn A (dark blue) cast on 31 sts and work in rib as follows:
Row 1 (RS): K2, [p1, k1] to last st, k1.
Row 2: P2, [k1, p1] to last st, p1.
Change to yarn B (light blue) and work 2 rows in rib, as rows 1–2.
Keep going in rib and work 4¾in (12cm).
Change color every two rows. End with a row 1.
Next row: Bind (cast) off 16 sts then rib (k1, p1) to the end of the row. (15 sts)
This part will be the flap for your case.
Work on these 15 sts for 1½in (4cm), ending with a row 2.
Bind (cast) off all stitches.

2 Sew the seams
Fold the knitted piece in half widthways, with the flap at the top.
Sew up the bottom and side seams.

3 Attach the loop

Work 2¼in (6cm) of finger-knitting. Thread your darning needle with yarn and sew the finger knitting to the center of the flap in a loop.

4

Pull down the loop over the case to find out where to put the button, and then sew it on—you may need to use an ordinary needle and thread if your darning needle won't go through the holes in the button.

Pompom necklace

It's fun and funky and this pompom necklace is really easy to make. The only knitting is finger knitting, which is a great way to begin. The tiny pompoms can be made with cardstock rings or pompom makers or try this really simple way using a dinner fork! Scraps of yarn from other projects are perfect for the pompoms.

You will need

....

Scraps of yarn in different colors

A fork with four prongs, or pompom maker with a diameter of about ¾in (2cm)

Sharp pointy scissors

Darning needle

Techniques (see pages 9–19)
Making pompoms (optional) see page 16

Finger knitting page 16

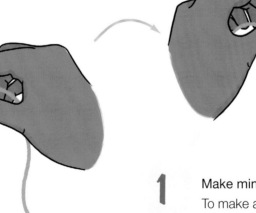

1 Make mini pompoms

To make a tiny pompom you can either use a small cardstock ring or pompom maker, or try this easy method. Wrap the yarn round and round the fork prongs until it gets really fat. Cut a small length of yarn and thread it through the middle gap in the fork and then tie it really tightly around all the wool you have wrapped.

Fluff up your POMPOMS!

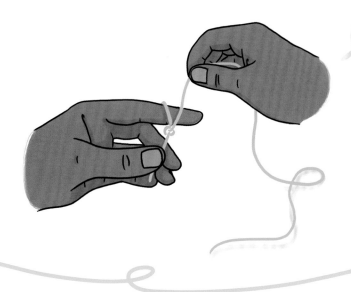

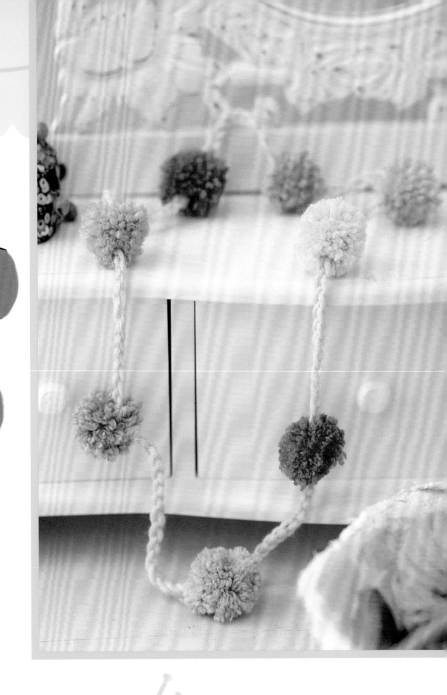

2 Pull the yarn off the fork. Push the blade of a small, sharp pair of scissors through all the loops on one side and snip them. Then do the same on the other side. Trim any long straggly bits and fluff up the pompom so that it is round and beautiful. Now make 6 or 7 more pompoms in different colors.

3 **Finger knit the chain**
Finger-knit a chain of approximately 24in (61cm) in a different color yarn. To finger knit, first make a slipknot in the yarn and slip it over your pointy/forefinger of the hand that you don't write with (so, the left finger if you are right-handed). Wrap another loop of yarn over your finger, closer to the end.

4 Holding the long end still with your second finger and thumb, with your right hand pull the first loop over the top of the second loop so you have one loop left on your finger.

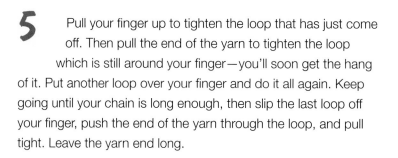

5 Pull your finger up to tighten the loop that has just come off. Then pull the end of the yarn to tighten the loop which is still around your finger—you'll soon get the hang of it. Put another loop over your finger and do it all again. Keep going until your chain is long enough, then slip the last loop off your finger, push the end of the yarn through the loop, and pull tight. Leave the yarn end long.

6 Thread on the pompoms
Thread the darning needle onto the tail of yarn on the finger knitting and carefully pull the needle through the center of each pompom. Space the pompoms evenly along the finger-knitted chain. Tie the ends of the finger knitting together using a knot or bow and trim the ends of yarn.

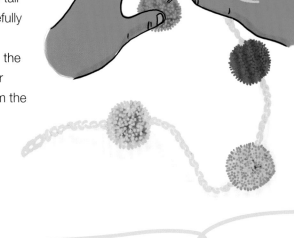

Ballet slippers

Pretty ballet slippers in which to dance your way to bed.
Did you ever dream that you could knit shoes?!

You will need

....

2(2:2) x 1¾oz (50g) balls—each
approx 127yd (116m)—Sublime
Cashmere Merino Silk DK (75% extra
fine merino, 20% silk, 5% cashmere),
in shade 009 pink

Pair of US 6 (4mm) knitting needles

Darning needle

Ribbon (2 pieces approx 20in/50cm
each)

Gauge (Tension)

22 sts and 28 rows to 4in (10cm) in
stockinette (stocking) stitch using US
6 (4mm) needles.

Finished size

Measure the length of your foot to
see which size you need.

Small 7in (19.5cm) long
Medium 7¾in (19.5cm) long
Large 8¼ (21cm) long

For the medium size follow the first
number in the brackets, for large the
second number. E.g Cast on
22(25:28) means cast on 22sts
for small, 25 for medium and 28
for large.

Abbreviations (see page 19)

Techniques (see pages 9–19)

Garter stitch page 12

Increasing page 13

Decreasing page 13

Sewing up page 15

---

1 Knit the basic slipper pattern

Using US 6 (4mm) needles
cast on 22(25:28) sts.
Work in garter st (every row knit),
increasing 1 st at either end of every
alternate row until there are
38(41:44) sts.
Work two rows straight.
Continue in garter st, decreasing 1 st
at either end of every alternate row
until you are back to 22(25:28) sts.
Cast on 8(10:10) sts at beginning of
next row for heel. (30[35:38] sts)
Continue in garter st, keeping heel
edge straight and increasing 1 st at
toe edge every alternate row until
there are 38(43:46) sts, ending at
heel edge.

Bind (cast) off 20(25:28) sts, knit to
end. (18 sts)
Knit 13(15:15) further rows on
remaining 18 sts, cast on 20(25:28)
sts at end of last row. (38[43:46] sts)
Keeping heel straight, work on
these sts, decreasing 1 st at toe
edge on every alternate row until
30(35:38) sts remain.
Bind (cast) off all sts.

Now cast on again and make
another one!

2 Using a darning needle and matching yarn, join the heel seam and edges around the sole, working in all the fullness at the toe.

3 Knit the heel tabs (make 2)
Cast on 8 sts and work 2½in (6cm) in garter st. Bind (cast) off all sts.

4 Sew each tab into a loop at the top of the heel. Thread a length of ribbon through each loop to tie around your ankles.

Perfect **SLIPPERS** for a prima ballerina

Tassel belt

This belt is really easy as it uses only the simplest knit stitch, but the stripes and tassels make it look like the work of an expert! A short version could be a scarf for a teddy or make it as long as you wish and in the colors you choose to accessorize your favorite outfit.

You will need

1 x 1¾oz (50g) ball—82yd (75m) of Aran weight yarn in each of 3 different colors, we used Debbie Bliss Eco Aran (100% organic cotton), in:

Yarn A: shade 620 lime
Yarn B: shade 609 purple
Yarn C: shade 621 jade

Pair of US 7 (4.5mm) knitting needles

Small crochet hook

Cardstock

Small, sharp pair of scissors

Darning needle

Finished size

You can make the belt any length to fit you, but with 10 stitches it is about 2¼in (6cm) wide. You could make it narrower or wider with different numbers of stitches.

Abbreviations (see page 19)

Techniques (see pages 9–19)

Garter stitch page 12

Changing color page 14

Weaving in ends page 15

1 Knit the belt

Using US 7 (4.5mm) needles and yarn A, cast on 10 stitches.

Row 1: Knit.

Row 2: Knit.

Change to yarn B.

Row 3: Knit.

Row 4: Knit.

Change to yarn C.

Row 5: Knit.

Row 6: Knit.

Change to yarn A.

Repeat these 6 rows, changing color every two rows until the belt is long enough to go round your waist and tie up with dangling ends. Finish the knitting with the Yarn A rows to make the two ends match. Bind (cast) off all stitches.

2 Use a darning needle to weave in all the ends, which will make the sides neat.

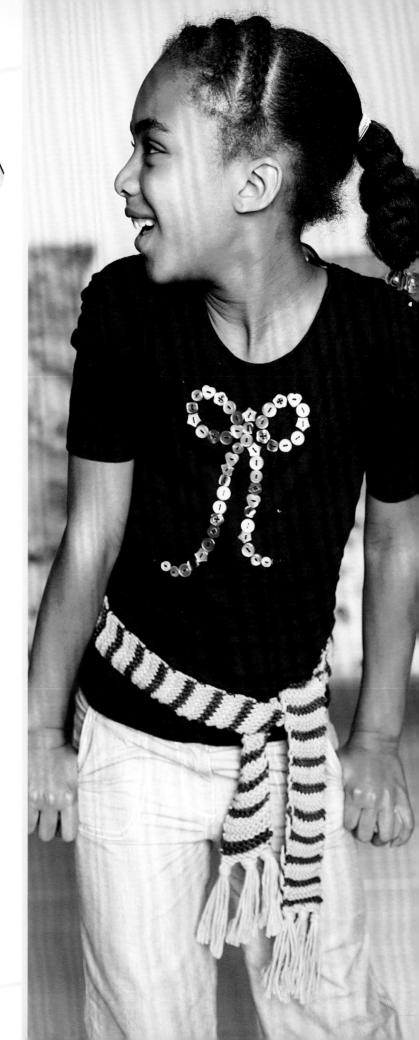

3 Make the tassels

Decide how long you want your tassels to be and cut a piece of cardstock to that length—about 4¾in (12cm) works well. Wind yarn A around the cardstock five times, starting and ending at the bottom of the card and cut it off. Push the point of a small, sharp pair of scissors through the loops at the bottom and cut the loops. Leave the yarn folded over the card at the top, lying it down with a book on top of it so it doesn't spring off the card.

4 Insert the crochet hook through the bottom right-hand corner of one end of the belt, then pick up the tassel strands where they fold, and catch the folds in the hook. Pull them through the belt for ½in (1cm) to make a loop. Now pass the cut ends of the tassel through the looped end and pull them tight.

5 Make 2 more tassels and add them to the end of the scarf, one in the center, and one in the opposite corner. Now make 3 more for the other end of the scarf. Trim any straggly or uneven ends of yarn so that the tassels are all the same length.

Tickly TASSELS

Heart key ring charm

Once you have made one of these cute little heart key rings you will realize just how quick and simple they are to knit. Then you could make lots of them—maybe to sell at a school fete or perhaps to give as presents to all your friends.

You will need

Any left-over DK weight yarn in a red shade, we used Sirdar Snuggly DK (55% nylon, 45% acrylic) in shade 413 engine red

Pair of US 6 (4mm) knitting needles

Small piece of narrow ribbon, about ¾in (2cm) long

Toy stuffing

Key ring

Darning needle

Sewing needle and red thread

Finished size

The heart is about 2in (5cm) wide

Abbreviations (see also page 19)

Inc increase
K2tog knit 2 stitches together
P2tog purl 2 stitches together

Techniques (see pages 9–19)

Increasing page 13

Decreasing page 13

Backstitch page 18

1 **Knit the heart**
Using US 6 (4mm) needles, cast on 3 sts.

Row 1: Purl.
Row 2: (right side) Inc1, knit to last st, inc1. (5 sts)
Repeat the last two rows until there are 15 sts.
Next row: Purl. (15 sts)
Work 4 rows straight in stockinette (stocking) stitch (one row knit, one row purl).
Next row: K2tog, k5, cast off 1 st, k5, k2tog. (12sts)
Next row: P4, p2tog, then turn the knitting to start another row. You will now have 6 stitches on the right needle, which you haven't knitted. Forget about these stitches and just keep knitting on the 5 stitches you have just worked. These will become one of the "bumps" at the top of the heart.
Next row: K2tog, k1, k2tog. (3 sts)
Next row: Purl.
Bind (cast) off.

Rejoin yarn to the remaining 6 sts that you left and work on these to make the second bump of the heart (which will match the first). To rejoin the yarn, insert your needle into the first stitch on the left needle, make a loop with the new yarn around the tip of the right needle, and work the stitch as normal.
Next row: P4, p2tog.

Next row: K2tog, k1, k2tog.
Next row: Purl.
Bind (cast) off and loosely tie the ends of together of the new yarn and the bound-off (cast-off) yarn to stop it unraveling.

Make another piece the same.

Attach the key ring

2 There will be a loop on your key ring for attaching the decoration. Thread the ribbon through this and pull it so that it is doubled over.

Sew the ribbon in place

3 With the wrong sides facing, pin the two heart pieces together, trapping the two ends of the ribbon between them at the top. Use the sewing needle and thread to stitch the ribbon in place sewing through all four layers with small backstitches.

Stuffing the heart

4 Now change to the darning needle and red yarn to sew around the rest of the heart with small neat overstitches, leaving a small gap at the end for stuffing. Keep your needle attached. Push small amounts of toy stuffing through the hole, you can use the wrong end of a pencil to help. When it is well shaped and plump, sew up the hole.

Pencil case

This stripy pencil case is ideal for that special set of pens or pencils. It is made from a simple rectangle of garter stitch, so no complicated increasing or decreasing is involved. It is lined with fabric to stop sharp points poking through.

You will need

1 x 1¾oz (50g) ball—approx 137yd (125m)—Rico Baby Cotton Soft DK (50% cotton, 50% acrylic), in each of:

Yarn A: shade 005 pistachio

Yarn B: shade 002 pink

Yarn C: shade 020 melon

Yarn D: shade 017 petrol

Yarn E: shade 015 yellow quartz

Pair of US 6 (4mm) knitting needles

Piece of cotton fabric, about 11 x 13in (28 x 33cm)

Sewing needle and thread

3 buttons

Finished size

About 9½ x 5½in (24 x14cm)

Abbreviations (see page 19)

Techniques (see pages 9–19)

Garter stitch page 12

Changing color page 14

Finger knitting page 16

Sewing buttons page 17

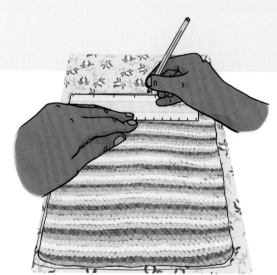

1 Knit the case

Using US 6 (4mm) needles and yarn A, cast on 52 sts.

Work in garter stitch (every row knit) on these 52 sts. Change color every two rows, keeping to the same sequence of colors. Keep knitting until the piece measures about 11½in (29cm) long. Bind (cast) off all sts.

Tip

Try a variegated or self-striping yarn to make the case even quicker to knit.

2 Cut out the lining

Place the knitted rectangle on top of the fabric. With a ruler and ball point pen, draw a rectangle around the knitting which is a little bigger than the knitting. Cut this out.

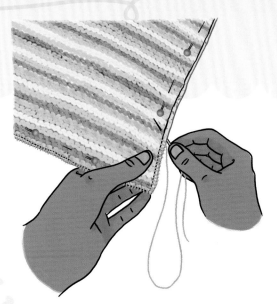

3 **Make the lining**

Ask an adult to help you use an iron to turn in a small hem all the way around the fabric so that it is the same size as the knitting. Pin the lining to the knitted piece with wrong sides together and sew them together using a sewing needle and overstitches. Make sure that you trap all the tails of yarn between the knitting and the lining.

4 Make up the pencil case

Fold the bottom edge up to make a pouch about 5in (13cm) deep, leaving a flap of about 1½in (3cm). Sew the side seams together using small overstitches.

5 Attach the button loops and buttons

Using the same color yarn as the edge of the flap, finger-knit 3 chains about 2in (5cm) long. Sew one loop about ¾in (2cm) in from the side of the flap at one end and one loop about ¾in (2cm) in from the side of the flap at the other end. Sew the last one in the middle. Fold down the flap to find where to put the buttons and then sew them on.

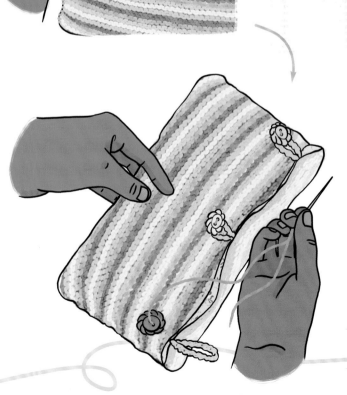

PERFECT for pencils

Chapter 3
Home Knits

Hot-water bottle cover 82

Patchwork blanket 84

Heart cushion 88

Caterpillar doorstop 90

Zigzag pillow 94

Toy basket 97

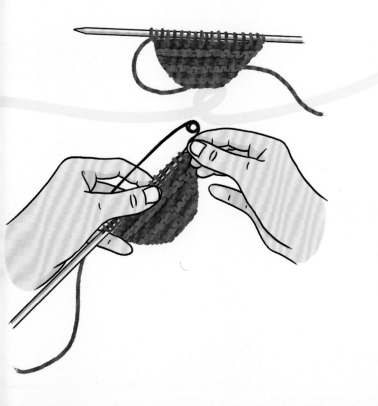

Hot-water bottle cover

On freezing cold nights what can be nicer than a hot-water bottle to warm up your bed and to cuddle as you go to sleep—but every hot-water bottle needs a soft cover. This one is made from a simple-to-knit rectangle. Knit it for yourself or make it for a pretty gift.

You will need

1 x 3½oz (100g) ball—approx 109yd (100m)—BC Garn Manu (100% baby alpaca), in each of:

Yarn A: shade un23 light teal

Yarn B: shade un05 dark teal

Pair of US 11 (8 mm) knitting needles

Darning needle

Approx 1yd (1m) of ½in (1cm) wide ribbon

Hot-water bottle

Finished size

This will fit an average hot-water bottle, which is about 9in wide x 14in high (23cm wide x 36cm high)

Techniques (see pages 9–19)

Garter stitch page 12

Stockinette (stocking) stitch page 12

Changing color page 14

Sewing up page 15

1 **Knit the cover**
Using US 11 (8mm) needles and yarn A (light blue), cast on 60 stitches.
Work 3in (7.5cm) in garter stitch (every row knit).
Change to yarn B (dark blue).
Next row: Purl.
Next row: Knit.
Continue in stockinette (stocking) stitch for 3in (7.5cm), ending with a purl row.
Change back to yarn A.
Work 8in (20cm) in garter stitch (every row knit).
Bind (cast) off all stitches.

2 **Sew up the seams**
Fold the knitted rectangle in half widthwise and sew up the bottom and side seam.

3   Thread the ribbon

Thread the ribbon in and out of the stitches, about 2½in (6.5cm) down from the opening. It's easier to thread ribbon if you wrap some sticky tape around the end to make it stiff. You can cut the tape off afterward.

Tip

Any bulky weight yarn will do, but try to find a soft and cozy yarn that you will enjoy cuddling and that will keep your bottle hot as long as possible.

Good night, SLEEP tight!

4

Slip the hot-water bottle into the cover, pull up the ribbon, and tie in a bow. Remember never to fill the hot-water bottle with hot water yourself—always ask an adult.

Patchwork blanket

A patchwork blanket made of squares is the perfect project when you are just starting out with knitting. You can try out different stitches in different squares and use up all sorts of oddments of yarn. You could even get all your friends knitting and make a really big blanket for someone who needs it. It's easier to sew up if all the squares are the same size, but it doesn't really matter if they're not!

You will need

You can use up any scraps of bulky or super bulky yarn to make this blanket. If you haven't got enough of one color to make a whole square, use it for stripes. And if you don't have any scraps, buy balls in the colors you like best.

Pair of US 13 (9mm) knitting needles

Darning needle

Finished size

Each square measures about 12 x 12in (30 x 30cm), so the whole blanket will be about 36in (90cm) wide and 48in (120cm) long

Techniques (see pages 9–19)

Garter stitch page 12

Stockinette (stocking) stitch page 12

Sewing up page 15

Weaving in yarn ends page 15

1 Knit the squares

Square one
Using US 13 (9mm) needles and any yarn you wish, cast on 30 stitches.
Work 12in (30cm) in garter stitch (every row knit). To test if it is square, fold the knitting from corner to corner—a square will fold perfectly in half. Bind (cast) off all stitches.

Square two
Using US 13 (9mm) needles and any yarn you wish, cast on 30 stitches.
Work 12in (30cm) in stockinette (stocking) stitch (one row knit, one row purl). Test that it is square. Bind (cast) off all stitches.

Make six of each square, in a mixture of colors, adding stripes if you wish
(see page 14).

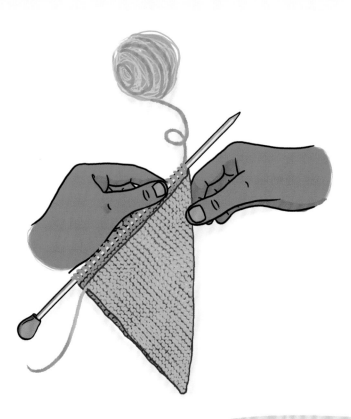

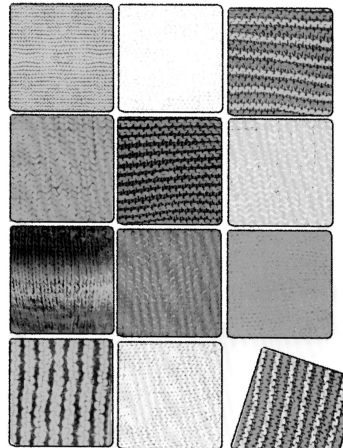

2 Sew up the squares
To sew up the squares, lay them all out flat and arrange them as you like, with three squares wide and four squares long. Try to arrange them with one side edge to a top or bottom edge (so the lines of knitting go in different directions) as this will help to neaten the squares.

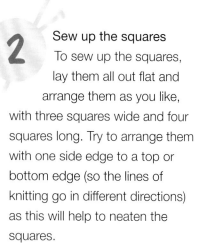

3 Using a yarn in a contrasting color, sew up the squares using overstitch or flat stitch. Sew in all the ends and, if your blanket isn't quite straight, ask an adult to help you to steam it very lightly into shape with an iron.

See how many SQUARES you can make!

Heart pillow

This pretty little heart shaped pillow would make a perfect gift for Mother's Day or Valentine's Day. You can stuff it in different ways: try sweet-smelling lavender if you plan to give it as a present for your mom or use a soft filling to make a cute accessory for your room.

You will need

1 x 1¾oz (50g) ball—approx 127yd (116m)—of Sublime Cashmere Merino Silk DK, (75% extra fine merino, 20% silk, 5% cashmere), in each of:

Yarn A: shade 159 pansy (purple)

Yarn B: shade 162 pinkaboo (pink)

Pair of US 6 (4mm) knitting needles

Stitch holder

Darning needle

Toy stuffing, beanbag beans, or dried lavender

Finished size

The heart will measure about 7¼in (18cm) wide and 6¼in (16cm) tall

Abbreviations (see also page 19)

Inc increase

K2tog knit to stitches together

Techniques (see pages 9–19)

Increasing page 13

Changing color page 14

Decreasing page 13

Garter stitch page 12

Sewing up page 15

1 **Knit the "bumps" of the heart**
Using US 6 (4mm) needles and yarn A (purple), cast on 5 sts.
Row 1: Knit.
Row 2: Inc1, knit to last st, inc1. (7 sts)
Change to yarn B (pink).
Repeat these two rows until you have 17 sts, changing color every two rows and ending with a row 2.
Break off these yarns and leave these 17 sts on a stitch holder.

Be my VALENTINE!

2 Join the two bumps

Make another piece the same as the one you have just made, but at the end keep this piece on the needle and don't break off the yarns. Instead, change yarn color as before, and knit the 17 stitches, then cast on one stitch. Now slide the 17 stitches on the stitch holder onto your left needle and knit across these as well. You will now have 35 stitches and the shaped top of the heart will be clear.

3 Finish the heart

Continue with the pattern below remembering to change color every two rows.

Next row: Knit
Next row: Inc1, knit to last st, inc1. (37 sts)
Next row: Knit one row.
Work the last two rows once more, then work in garter stitch for eight rows. (39 sts)
Next row: K2tog, knit to last 2 sts, k2tog. (37 sts)
Work 3 rows garter stitch.
Repeat last 4 rows twice more. (33 sts)
Next row: K2tog, knit to last 2sts, k2tog. (31 sts)
Next row: Knit one row.
Repeat last two rows until 3 sts remain.
Next row: K3tog.
Fasten off yarn (cut off the yarn and pass it through the last stitch and pull tight).
Now knit another heart using all yarn B (pink).

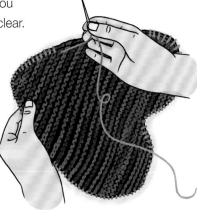

4 Sew the heart together

Sew together the two pieces, leaving a small gap in the side seam for stuffing.

5 Stuff the heart

Fill the heart with toy stuffing or your chosen filling until it is well shaped and firm, then sew up the gap.

Caterpillar doorstop

You could use this stripy caterpillar as a doorstop or draft excluder, but he'll probably be too cute to leave on the floor and he will deserve a place on your bed instead.

You will need

1 x 1¾oz (50g) ball—approx 87yd (80m)—Debbie Bliss Rialto Aran (100% merino wool), in each of:

Yarn A: shade 22 pale green
Yarn B: shade 10 green
Yarn C: shade 23 baby blue
Yarn D: shade 18 red

Pair of US 8 (5mm) knitting needles

Darning needle

Toy stuffing

Pompom cardstock rings or pompom maker

Buttons for eyes

Finished size

The caterpillar will end up about 26½in (67cm) long

Abbreviations (see also page 19)

Inc   increasing
K2tog knit 2 stitches together
St st stockinette (stocking) stitch

Techniques (see pages 9–19)

Inc1 page 13

Increasing page 13

Changing color page 14

Decreasing page 13

Sewing up page 15

Making pompoms page 16

Sewing buttons page 17

Embroidery stitches pages 17–18

1 Knit the body

Using US 8 (5mm) needles, and yarn A, cast on 5 sts.

Row 1 (and every other row): Purl.
Row 2: Inc1 into each st to end of row. (10 sts)
Row 4: Inc1 twice into each st to end of row. (20 sts)
Row 6: [K1, inc1] to end of row. (30 sts)
Row 8: [K2, inc1] to end of row. (40 sts)
Row 10: [K3, inc1] to end of row. (50 sts)
Work ¾in (2cm) st st straight in yarn A.
Change to yarn B and work ¾in (2cm) st st straight.
Change to yarn C and work ¾in (2cm) st st straight.

Continue in st st in alternating ¾in (2cm) stripes of three colors until the caterpillar measures approx 25in (63.5cm). End with a purl row and a complete stripe.
Change color for the next stripe and keep to this color until the end.
Next row: [K3, k2tog] to end of row. (40 sts)
Next row (and every other row): Purl.
Next row: [K2, k2tog] to end of row. (30 sts)
Next row: [K1, k2tog] to end of row. (20 sts)
Next row: [K2tog] to end of row. (10 sts)
Next row: [K2tog] to end of row. (5 sts)
Do not bind (cast) off, but thread the tail end through the remaining stitches, pull up tight to make a circle, and secure it with a few stitches.

A ROLY POLY caterpillar

Tip

You could make a multicolored version using up old scraps of yarn.

2 Sew the seam

Sew up the side seam, leaving a gap in the middle of the seam about 4in (10cm) long to stuff. Push toy stuffing through the gap into the tube. Use the handle of a wooden spoon to push the stuffing right up to the ends of the caterpillar and then stuff the rest of the body until it is firm and well shaped. Sew up the gap.

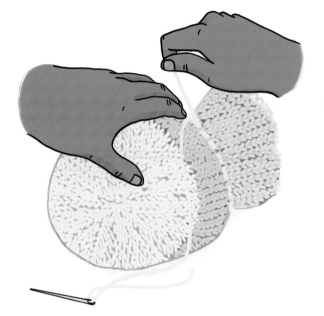

3 **Make the head and tail**
Thread a length of yarn on a darning needle. About 4in (10cm) from one end stitch a few small stitches over and over in one place to secure the yarn, then stitch right around the caterpillar in running stitches with each stitch about ½in (1cm) long. At the end pull the yarn gently to pull in a neck for the caterpillar's head. Secure the yarn with a few more stitches over and over. Do the same at the other end to make a tail.

4 **Knit the legs (make eight, or more!)**
Using US 8 (5mm) needles and yarn D, cast on 8 sts.
Work ¾in (2cm) in garter st.
Bind (cast) off 4 sts, work straight in garter st on these 4 sts for a further ¾in (2cm).
Bind (cast) off all sts.

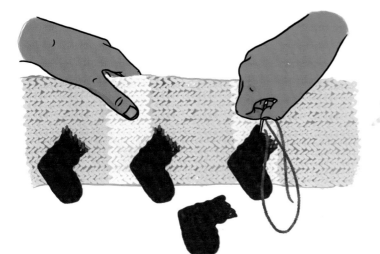

5 Attach the legs

Using matching yarn, sew the legs to the body, spacing them out evenly on both sides between the head and tail.

6 Finish the head

Make two pompoms, we used 2 colors of yarn, and attach them to the head for antennae.

7

Sew on two buttons for eyes, and embroider a nose and smile using long straight stitches in yarn D (red).

Zigzag pillow

The knitting in this pillow looks hard but it's actually fun and easy. Learning to knit the stripes will teach you how to shape your knitting—each color is one strip with the zigzags created by increasing and decreasing the number of stitches. Knit the stripes in all the colors of the rainbow!

You will need

1 x 1¾oz (50g) ball—approx 127yd (116m)—Sublime Cashmere Merino Silk DK (75% extra fine merino, 20% silk, 5% cashmere), in each of:

Yarn A: shade 119 lido

Yarn B: shade 124 splash

Yarn C: shade 194 seesaw

Yarn D: shade 195 puzzle

Yarn E: shade 122 honeybunny

Yarn F: shade 158 ladybug

Yarn G: shade td53 purple

Pair of US 6 (4mm) knitting needles

Darning needle

12 x 12in (30 x 30cm) pillow form (cushion pad)

Finished size

The finished cushion is about 12 x 12in (30 x 30cm)

Abbreviations (see also page 19)

Inc increase

K2tog knit 2 stitches together

RS right side

Techniques (see pages 9–19)

Increasing page 13

Decreasing page 13

Sewing up page 15

1 Knit the zigzag strips
Strip 1: you will need four zigzag strips like this—all in different colors.

Using US 6 (4mm) needles and yarn A, cast on 6 sts.
Row 1 (RS): Knit.
Row 2: Purl.
**Row 3: K2, inc1, knit to last two sts, inc1, k2.
Row 4: Purl.
Repeat rows 3–4 until you have 16 sts, ending with a purl row.
Next row: K2, k2tog, knit to last 4 sts, k2tog, k2.
Next row: Purl.
Repeat the last two rows until you have 6 sts, ending with a purl row.**

Repeat from ** to ** eight more times, so you have nine full repeats.
Bind (cast) off all sts.
Make three more strips, one in each of yarns C, E, and G.

Strip 2: you will need 3 zigzag strips like this—all in different colors.

Using US 6 (4mm) needles, and yarn B, cast on 16 sts.
Row 1 (RS): Knit.
Row 2: Purl.
**Row 3: K2, k2tog, knit to last four sts, k2tog, k2.
Row 4: Purl.
Repeat rows 3–4 until you have 6 sts, ending with a purl row.
Next row: K2, inc1, knit to last 2 sts, inc1, k2.
Next row: Purl.
Repeat last two rows until you have 16 sts, ending with a purl row.**

Repeat from ** to ** eight more times, so you have nine full repeats.
Bind (cast) off all sts.
Make two more strips, one in each of yarns D and F.

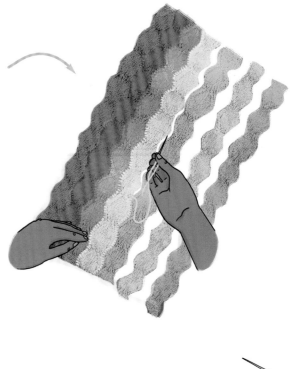

2

Assemble the strips

Lay out all the 7 strips in alphabetical order A to G, and with the right side facing down. Sew all the strips together on the back with whip stitch, so that the zigzags fit together and the top and bottom are straight.

Multicolored STYLE

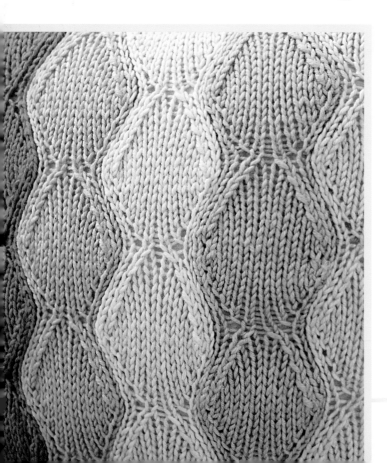

3

Finish the pillow

Place the knitted piece over the front of the pillow form and fold it over to the back across the middle. Sew up the three side seams with whip stitch and matching yarn.

Toy basket

This patchwork bag is all made from rectangles so it's simple to knit and, as it is knitted in super bulky yarn, it grows super quickly. The yarn is fabric yarn, which makes a good solid bag for holding toys or other bits and pieces. With a few bags like this you'll soon tidy up your own or a toddler's bedroom!

You will need

1 x 28oz/800g cone—approx 130yd (120m)—DMC Hoooked Zpagetti (92% recycled cotton, 8% other recycled fibers), in each of 3 colors, we used:

Yarn A: green
Yarn B: red
Yarn C: dark blue

Pair each of US 17 (12mm) and US 11 (8mm) knitting needles

Darning needle

Finished size

The basket measures about 12in long x 12in wide x 10in high (30cm long x 30cm wide x 25cm high)

Abbreviations (see page 19)

Techniques (see pages 9–19)

Garter stitch page 12

Sewing up page 15

 1 Knit the base
Using US 17 (12mm) needles and yarn A (green), cast on 23 stitches and work in garter stitch (every row knit) until the knitting measures 12in (30cm) long. Bind (cast) off.
Make another piece the same.

2 Knit the sides
Using US 17 (12mm) needles and yarn B (red), cast on 21 stitches and work in garter stitch (every row knit) until the knitting measures 12in (30cm) long. Bind (cast) off.
Work one more piece the same in yarn B and 2 more in yarn C (blue).
You will now have 5 rectangles of knitting.

 3 Knit the handles
Using US 11 (8mm) needles and yarn B (red), cast on 5 stitches and work in garter stitch (every row knit) until the handle measures about 14in (35cm) long. Knit another handle the same.

4 Sew the basket together

Sew the long sides of the red rectangles to opposite sides of the green rectangle. Now sew the long sides of the blue rectangles to the other two sides of the green rectangle so that you have a cross shape. Lift up a red and a blue piece and stitch the sides together to make the first corner of a box shape. Do the same for the other three corners.

5

Attach a handle to the top edge of each red side, sewing on the ends about 2in (5cm) in from the edges of the square, sewing them with overstitches where the edges meet. Make sure the handle isn't twisted before you sew.

Tidy up those TOYS

Chapter 4

Fun Knits

Sheriff's star badge 102

Ladybug buddies 104

Doctor's stethoscope 106

Baby ball 108

Teddy bear 110

Pirate flag 114

Cute alien 117

Rag doll 120

Sheriff's star badge

Every town needs a sheriff to keep an eye on things, so knit yourself a star, pin it to your chest, wear it with a cowboy hat, and chase the bank robbers outta town! Or, if you are not into cowboys, why not knit yourself a star to hang on the Christmas tree instead? Decorate it with sequins!

You will need

Small amount of yellow DK/worsted weight yarn

Pair of US 5 (3.75mm) knitting needles

Darning needle

Scraps of yarn for embroidery

Toy stuffing

Sewing needle and thread

Safety pin or brooch back

Finished size

The star is about 4in (10cm) in diameter

Abbreviations (see also page 19)

Inc increase

K2tog knit 2 stitches together

Techniques (see pages 9–19)

Increasing page 13

Decreasing page 13

Embroidery stitches pages 17–18

Sewing up page 15

1 **Knit the star**
The star is made of 5 diamonds stitched together. It needs a front and a back so you need to knit 10 diamonds altogether.

Using US 5 (3.75mm) needles, cast on 3 sts.
Next row: Inc1, knit to last st, inc1.
Next row: Purl.
Repeat the last two rows until there are 11 sts, ending with a purl row.
Next row: K2tog, knit to last 2 sts, k2tog.
Next row: Purl.
Repeat the last two rows until 3 sts remain, ending with a purl row.
Next row: K3tog.
Fasten off yarn.

2 Sew 5 pieces together in a circle, joining the lower sides of the diamond shapes together. Do the same with the other 5 pieces so that you have two stars.

Tip

Try some metallic yarns to make it look like a real metal star!

3 On the right side of one star, using a different color yarn, embroider an "S" with simple straight or running stitches.

Watch out for the SHERIFF!

4 With wrong sides together and the "S" on the outside, sew the two stars together. Leave a small gap for stuffing. Keep your needle and thread still attached.

5 Push small amounts of toy stuffing into the badge through the gap. Use the wrong end of a pencil to push it up into the points of the star. When the star is well shaped and firm, sew up the gap.

6 Sew a brooch back or safety pin onto the back of the badge, using a sewing needle and thread and lots of small stitches. Make sure that you secure the thread by sewing a few small stitches over and over in one place.

Ladybug buddies

Make a cute little ladybug family to line up on a shelf. This is a great project to help you learn new techniques like increasing and knitting together and how to use a pattern. Have a pencil nearby as you knit, and tick off each row on the pattern as you complete it, to help you keep track of where you are.

You will need

Small amounts of DK or sportweight yarn in red or pink, we used Millamia Merino (100% merino wool), in:

Large bug: shade 140 scarlet (A)

Small bug: shade 143 fuchsia (B)

Small amount of DK or sportweight yarn in black, we used Rico Essentials Merino DK (100% merino wool), in shade 90 black (C)

Pair of US 5 (3.75mm) knitting needles

4 white buttons for eyes

Assorted black buttons for spots (or you could make spots from circles of felt)

Toy stuffing

Darning needle

Sewing needle and thread

Finished size

Large bug: approx 4in (10cm) wide

Small bug: approx 2½in (6.5cm) wide

Abbreviations (see also page 19)

Inc increase
K2tog knit 2 stitches together
Dec Decrease

Techniques (see pages 9–19)

Increasing page 13

Decreasing page 13

Changing color page 14

Sewing buttons page 17

Sewing up page 15

1

Knit the large ladybug

This is made with garter stitch which means all rows knit. You will need to knit two pieces the same shape—the belly, which is knitted all in red, and the back, which is half red and half black.

For both belly and back:

Using US 5 (3.75mm) needles and yarn A (red), cast on 5 sts.

Row 1: Knit.
Row 2: Cast on 3 sts, knit to end of row. (8 sts)
Row 3: Cast on 3 sts, knit to end of row. (11 sts)
Rows 4 and 5: Garter st without increasing.
Row 6: Cast on 3 sts, knit to end of row. (14 sts)
Row 7: Cast on 3 sts, knit to end of row. (17 sts)
Rows 8, 9, 10, 11: Garter stitch without increasing.
Row 12: Cast on 2 sts, knit to end of row. (19 sts)
Row 13: Cast on 2 sts, knit to end of row. (21 sts)
Rows 14, 15, 16, 17, 18: Garter st without increasing.

Row 19: Inc1 at either end of row. (23 sts)
Rows 20, 21, 22, 23, 24, 25, 26: Garter st without increasing.
Row 27: K2tog at either end of row. (21 sts)

For the belly continue in yarn A (red). For the back now change to yarn C (black).

Rows 28, 29, 30, 31, 32: Garter st without decreasing.
Row 33: Bind (cast) off 2 sts, knit to end of row. (19 sts)
Row 34: Bind (cast) off 2 sts, knit to end of row. (17 sts)
Rows 35, 36, 37, 38: Garter st without decreasing.
Row 39: Bind (cast) off 3 sts, knit to end of row. (14 sts)
Row 40: Bind (cast) off 3 sts, knit to end of row. (11 sts)
Rows 41 and 42: Garter st without decreasing.
Row 43: Bind (cast) off 3 sts, knit to end of row. (8 sts)
Row 44: Bind (cast) off 3 sts, knit to end of row. (5 sts)
Row 45: Knit.
Bind (cast) off all sts.

2 Knit the small ladybug

This is just like the large ladybug—it is all knitted in garter stitch (all rows knit). You will need to knit two pieces the same shape—the belly, which is knitted all in pink, and the back, which is half pink and half black.

For both belly and back:
Using US 5 (3.75mm) needles and yarn B (pink), cast on 3 sts.

Row 1: Knit.
Row 2: Cast on 3 sts, knit to end of row. (6 sts)
Row 3: Cast on 3 sts, knit to end of row. (9 sts)
Rows 4, 5: Garter st without increasing.
Row 6: Cast on 2 sts, knit to end of row. (11 sts)
Row 7: Cast on 2 sts, knit to end of row. (13 sts)
Rows 8, 9, 10, 11: Garter st without increasing.
Row 12: Inc 1 st at either end of row. (15 sts)
Rows 13, 14, 15, 16, 17: Garter st without increasing.
Row 18: Dec 1 st at either end of row. (13 sts)

For the belly continue in yarn B (pink). For the back now change to yarn C (black).

Rows 19, 20, 21, 22: Garter st without decreasing.
Row 23: Bind (cast) off 2 sts, knit to end of row. (11 sts)
Row 24: Bind (cast) off 2 sts, knit to end of row. (9 sts)
Rows 25 and 26: Garter st without decreasing.
Row 27: Bind (cast) off 3 sts, knit to end of row. (6 sts)
Row 28: Bind (cast) off 3 sts, knit to end of row. (3 sts)
Row 29: Knit.
Bind (cast) off all 3 stitches.

SPOTS galore!

3 Add the eyes and spots

Take the back piece and sew black buttons on the red/pink half for spots and white buttons on the black half for eyes. Add a few stitches in red or pink yarn for the mouth.

4 Sew the bug

Sew the belly and back pieces together all round the edge using a darning needle and red or pink yarn, leaving a gap of about ½in (1cm) for stuffing. Keep your needle attached. Push toy stuffing through the gap, until each ladybug is firm and fat. Sew up the gap.

Doctor's stethoscope

Make yourself a French-knitted stethoscope for dressing up as a doctor or nurse and check that all your toys are in the best of health!

You will need

1 x 1¾oz (50g)—approx 127yd (116m)—Sublime Cashmere Merino Silk DK (75% merino, 20% silk, 5% cashmere), in shade td53 purple

French knitting bobbin

Darning needle

Large button

Finished size

About 16in (40cm) long

Techniques (see page 19)

French knitting page 17

Sewing buttons page 17

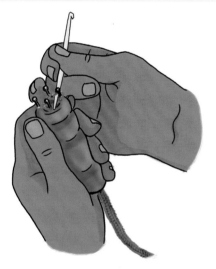

1 Knit the stethoscope

Following the instructions included with the bobbin, French knit two tubes, one 8in (20cm) long and one 16in (40cm) long.

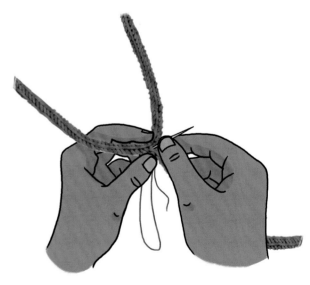

2 Join the stethoscope

Fold the longer tube into a "U" shape and sew the shorter tube to the center bottom of the "U" tube using a darning needle and matching yarn.

Take a deep BREATH!

3 Add the button
Sew the large button to the bottom of the short tube so that it dangles down.

4 Add the ear loops
Cut a length of yarn long enough to loop over your ears. Cut a second piece of yarn to the same length. Sew a loop of yarn to either end of the "U" tube, making sure you secure the ends with several stitches. You're now ready for any emergency!

Baby ball

Is there a toddler or a new baby in your family? This colorful ball is a perfect first ball for a baby to play with. It's soft so they can grip it, it's light so they can roll it and catch it, and if you hang it from a ribbon above their crib they can bat it around. A perfect gift for a baby but it's also pretty good for playing with yourself!

You will need

1 x 1¾oz (50g) ball—approx 137yd (125m)—DK weight yarn in 3 colors, we used Millamia Merino (100% merino), in:

Yarn A: shade 140 scarlet

Yarn B: shade 141 grass

Yarn C: shade 144 peacock

Pair of US 5 (3.75mm) knitting needles

Darning needle

Toy stuffing

Finished size

About 12in (30cm) around widest part

Abbreviations (see also page 19)

Inc increase
K2tog knit 2 stitches together
St st stockinette (stocking) stitch

Techniques (see pages 9–19)

Increasing page 13

Decreasing page 13

Sewing up page 15

---

1 Knit the segments

(Have a pencil handy to tick off each row as you finish it.)

Using US 5 (3.75mm) needles and yarn A (red), cast on 3 sts.

Row 1: Inc1, k1, inc1. (5 sts)
Row 2: Purl.
Row 3: Inc1, knit to last st, inc1. (7 sts)
Row 4: Purl.
Row 5: Inc1, knit to last st, inc1. (9 sts)
Work 3 rows st st.
Row 9: Inc, knit to last st, inc1. (11 sts)
Work 5 rows st st.
Row 15: Inc1, knit to last st, inc1. (13 sts)
Work 15 rows st st.

Row 31: K2tog, knit to last 2 sts, k2tog. (11 sts)
Work 5 rows st st.
Row 37: K2tog, knit to last 2 sts, k2tog. (9 sts)
Work 3 rows st st.
Row 41: K2tog, knit to last 2 sts, k2tog. (7 sts)
Row 42: Purl.
Row 43: K2tog, knit to last 2 sts, k2tog. (5 sts)
Row 44: Purl.
Row 45: K2tog, k1, k2tog. (3 sts)
Bind (cast) off all sts.

Make one more segment in red, (yarn A), 2 segments in blue (yarn B), and 2 segments in green (yarn C).

2 Sew the ball

Lay the six segments out in a row with alternating colors—red, green, blue, red, green, blue. Join each segment to the next along the long sides. Only sew up half of the last seam to leave a gap for stuffing. Keep your needle and yarn attached.

CATCH me if you can!

3 Stuff the ball

Push small pieces of toy stuffing into the ball until it is round and firm, then sew up the gap.

Teddy bear

Everyone has a favorite toy and this cute teddy, with his smiley little face and squishy body, is bound to become yours. The furry yarn we used is perfect for a bear because it is incredibly soft and cozy, but you could experiment with other textures. Using a machine washable yarn is a good idea because favorite teddies get very grubby and will need to be washed from time to time.

You will need

1 x 1¾oz (50g) ball—approx 137yd (125m)—of Regia Softy (39% new wool, 61% polyamide), in shade 435 beige

Pair of US 6 (4mm) knitting needles

Darning needle

Toy stuffing

Buttons for eyes

Ribbon for decoration

Oddments of embroidery floss (thread) or yarn for face

Finished size

About 11in (28cm) high

Abbreviations (see also page 19)

K2tog knit 2 stitches together
St st stockinette (stocking) stitch

Techniques (see pages 9–19)

Stockinette (stocking) stitch page 12

Sewing up page 15

Decreasing page 13

Sewing buttons page 17

Embroidery stitches pages 17–18

1 Knit the legs (make 2)
Leaving a long tail of wool (which you will need later) and using US 6 (4mm) needles, cast on 20 sts and work 4¼in (11cm) in st st (one row knit, one row purl). Do not bind (cast) off.
Cut yarn and thread it onto a darning needle then thread it through the remaining stitches.

Pull it up tight to close the end. Decide which side will be the outside and then sew the side seam together to form a tube and stuff the leg with toy stuffing until it is firm and well shaped. Thread the long tail at the open end (that you left when you were casting on), onto a darning needle, then thread the yarn in and out all around the cast-on edge of the leg (like sewing a running stitch using quite small stitches). Pull up tight to close the leg and then secure the yarn with a few stitches over and over in the same place.

2 Knit the arms (make 2)
Leaving a long tail of yarn and using US 6 (4mm) needles, cast on 16 sts and work 3¼in (8cm) in st st. Do not bind (cast) off.
Cut yarn and thread it onto a darning needle then through the remaining sts, pulling up tight to close the end. Decide if you want the same side outside for the arms as for the legs then sew the side seam together to form a tube. Stuff and finish each arm like you did for the legs in step 1.

Tip

You can use either side of the knitting as the right side on this pattern, or a mixture of both, as here, to use both textures—each looks good in this furry yarn.

3 Knit the body

Using US 6 (4mm) needles, cast on 50 sts and work 4¼in (11cm) in st st.

Do not bind (cast) off.

Cut yarn and thread it onto a darning needle then through the remaining sts, pulling up tight to close the end.

Decide which side you want outside for the body and for the head and sew the side seam together to form a tube. Stuff and finish it like you did for the legs in step 1.

A cute, cuddly TEDDY BEAR

4 Knit the head

Leaving a long tail of yarn and using US 6 (4mm) needles, cast on 60 sts and work 3½in (9cm) in st st.

Do not bind (cast) off.

Cut yarn and thread it onto a darning needle then through the remaining sts, pulling up tight to close the end. Sew the side seam together, then stuff and finish it like you did for the legs in step 1.

5 Knit the ears

Using US 6 (4mm) needles, cast on 9 sts.

Knit one row.

Next row: K2tog, knit to last 2 sts, k2tog.

Repeat the last two rows until 5 sts remain.

Knit one row.

Bind (cast) off all sts.

6 Sew teddy together

Using a darning needle and yarn, sew the head and arms and legs to the body with lots of overstitches all the way round. Each time you sew make sure that you secure the thread well when you begin and when you finish by sewing a few stitches over and over in one place.

7 Add teddy's features

Using a darning needle and yarn, sew the ears to the head. Then sew buttons for eyes and embroider on a mouth and nose with a few straight stitches. Tie a piece of ribbon around teddy's neck for the finishing touch.

Pirate flag

What do pirates do when they are in the middle of the sea and there's no treasure in sight? Knit flags! This one is a simple rectangle in stockinette (stocking) stitch with garter stitch edges so it doesn't curl up. The skull and crossbones are made of felt. You can use our template or create your own scary skull!

You will need

2 x 1¾oz (50g) balls—approx 123yd (113m) any DK weight yarn in black, we used Rowan Wool Cotton (50% merino wool, 50% cotton) in shade 908 inky

Pair of US 6 (4mm) knitting needles

Paper for template and pencil

Sharp pointed scissors

Templates on page 125

Piece of white felt, about 8in (20cm) square

Sewing needle and red thread

Small amount of white yarn

Finished size

The flag is about 16 x 12in (40 x 30cm)

Abbreviations (see page 19)

Techniques (see pages 9–19)

Garter stitch page 12

Stockinette (stocking) stitch page 12

Finger knitting page 16

Embroidery stitches pages 17–18

1 **Knit the flag**
Using US 6 (4mm) needles, cast on 81 sts. Work 11 rows garter stitch (every row knit).
Row 12: K9, purl to last 9 sts, k9.
Row 13: Knit.
Repeat the last two rows until the flag measures about 10½in (27cm) ending with row 13. Work 10 rows in garter stitch.
Bind (cast) off all stitches.

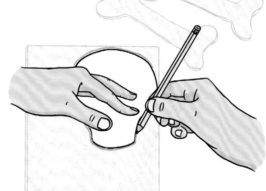

2 **Make the skull and crossbones**
Trace the skull and crossbones templates on page 125 onto paper and cut them out. Pin the templates to the felt, and draw around them. Draw around the bone again. Cut out the shapes. To cut out the eyes, mouth, and nose, make a small snip in the middle of the shape then cut to the line.

3 Pin the skull and crossbones to the center of the flag, crossing the bones to make an "X" shape. Blanket stitch the shapes in place with sewing needle and red thread.

4 Finger-knit two ties, about 24in (60cm) long from white yarn. Fold one tie in half to find the middle and then sew the middle point to the top left corner of the flag with a sewing needle and thread and small stitches. Do the same with the other tie, sewing it to the bottom left corner of the flag.

SHIVER me timbers!

Cute alien

This cute little alien toy has a furry head! Make it as weird and wonderful as you like with fangs, tentacles, and as many eyes as an alien needs!

You will need

1 x 1¾oz (50g) ball—approx 71yd (65m)—Sirdar Escape Wool Rich Chunky (51% wool, 49% acrylic) in shade 197 (A)

1 x 1¾oz (50g) ball—approx 43yd (40m)—Gedifra Antiga (34% acrylic, 30% polyamide, 18% mohair, 18% wool), in shade 3101 (B)

Pair of US 11 (8mm) knitting needles

Large-eyed needle with a point sharp enough to sew through felt

Toy stuffing

Sewing needle and thread

Felt for arms and legs

Buttons for eyes

Finished size

About 8in (20cm) at widest point

Abbreviations (see also page 19)

Inc   increase
k2tog   knit 2 stitches together

Techniques (see pages 9–19)

Garter stitch page 12
Increasing page 13
Decreasing page 13
Changing color page 14
Sewing up page 15
Sewing buttons page 17

1 Knit the front of the body

Using yarn A and US 11 (8mm) needles, cast on 12 sts.

Row 1: Knit.
Row 2: Inc1, knit to last st, inc1. (14 sts)
Repeat the last 2 rows until you have 22 sts.
Work straight in garter st until work measures 3¼in (8cm) from cast-on edge.
Change to yarn B (furry) and work 2in (5cm) in garter st.
Next row: K2tog, knit to last 2 sts, k2tog. (20 sts)
Next row: Knit.
Repeat last 2 rows once more. (18 sts)
Continue on these 18 sts for 1¼in (3cm).
Next row: Knit 4 stitches. Then turn the knitting to start another row leaving 14 stitches on the needle that you haven't knitted. Forget about these stitches and just keep knitting on the four stitches.
Work 4 rows garter st on these 4 sts.
Next row: [K2tog] twice. (2 sts)
Next row: Knit.
Next row: K2tog, fasten off yarn.

This will have created a point for the alien's head. You need three more points so you will need to do the same thing again three times so:

Rejoin yarn to remaining 14 stitches, k5 stitches then turn, leaving remaining 9 stitches unworked on the needle.
Work 4 rows garter st on these 5 sts.
Next row: K2tog, k1, k2tog. (3 sts)
Next row: Knit.
Next row: K3tog, fasten off yarn.

Rejoin yarn to remaining 9 sts, k5, turn, leaving remaining 4 stitches unworked.
Work 4 rows garter st on these 5 sts.
Next row: K2tog, k1, k2tog. (3 sts)
Next row: Knit.
Next row: K3tog, fasten off yarn.
Rejoin yarn to remaining 4 sts, k4.
Work 4 further rows garter st on these 4 sts.
Next row: [K2tog] twice. (2 sts)
Next row: Knit.
Next row: K2tog, fasten off yarn.

Now knit the back of the body in the same way.

2 Cut out the felt arms and legs

Draw an arm shape on a piece of paper and cut it out to make a template. Do the same for the leg shape but make it slightly larger. Trace round your templates to cut out four felt pieces for the arms and four for the legs.

3 Sew the arms and legs

Place two arm pieces together and sew them around the edge with a neat overstitch, leaving one seam open for stuffing. Keep the needle attached. Fill the arm shape with pieces of toy stuffing until it is nice and firm, then sew up the gap. Repeat with the other arm piece and the legs.

4 Sew the body

Pin the two body pieces together with the arms and legs pinned into place between them. Sew the two body pieces together using a darning needle and matching yarn. Use whip stitch around the head and body but when you come to the arms and legs use back stitch through all four layers to sew them securely in place. Leave a small gap in one side for stuffing. Keep your needle and yarn attached.

Crazy CRITTERS

5 **Finishing the alien**

Fill the body of the alien with small tufts of toy stuffing until it is nice and firm. Use the wrong end of a pencil to push the stuffing up into the points of the head. Then sew up the gap. Sew on eyes to the un-furry part of the body. You can also embroider a mouth and any other weird or scary features you want.

Rag doll

Every rag doll is different and special but a rag doll you have knitted yourself will become a very special friend. You can make her in your favorite colors and give her a smile that is just for you.

You will need

1 x 1¾oz (50g) ball—approx 84yd (77m)—Mission Falls 1824 cotton (100% cotton), in each of:

Yarn A: shade 200 biscuit
Yarn B: shade 407 aubergine
Yarn C: shade 202 cardinal
Yarn D: shade 302 green
Pair of US 7 (4.5mm) knitting needles

Darning needle

Large safety pin

Toy stuffing

Scraps of felt for cheeks

Sewing needle and thread

Buttons for eyes and for dress

Finished size

About 23in (58.5cm) tall

Abbreviations (see also page 19)

Inc increase
K2tog knit 2 stitches together
St st stockinette (stocking) stitch

Techniques (see pages 9–19)

Stockinette (stocking) stitch page 12

Increasing page 13

Decreasing page 13

Sewing up page 15

Changing color page 14

Sewing buttons page 17

Embroidery stitches pages 17–18

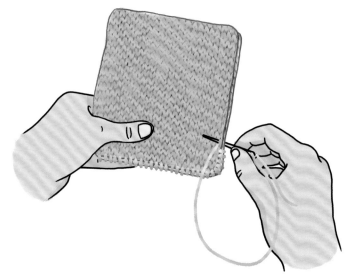

1 Knit the body

Using US 7 (4.5mm) needles and yarn A (brown), cast on 40 sts. Work 5½in (14cm) in st st. Bind (cast) off all sts.

Fold the piece in half widthwise and sew up two of the seams. Fill the body with small pieces of toy stuffing until it is well shaped then sew up the remaining seam.

Knit your own **SPECIAL** friend

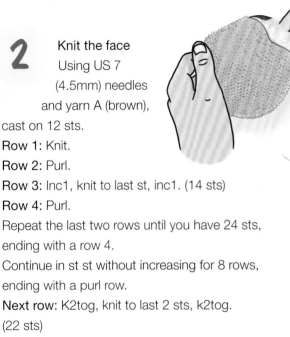

2 Knit the face

Using US 7 (4.5mm) needles and yarn A (brown), cast on 12 sts.

Row 1: Knit.
Row 2: Purl.
Row 3: Inc1, knit to last st, inc1. (14 sts)
Row 4: Purl.
Repeat the last two rows until you have 24 sts, ending with a row 4.
Continue in st st without increasing for 8 rows, ending with a purl row.
Next row: K2tog, knit to last 2 sts, k2tog. (22 sts)
Next row: Purl.
Repeat the last two rows until you have 12 sts. Bind (cast) off all sts.

Make another piece the same for the back of the head, using yarn B (purple). Sew the two pieces together all round the edge, with the purl side as the right side for the back of the head and the knit side as right side for the face. Leave a small gap for stuffing and leave your needle attached. Fill the head with small pieces of toy stuffing until it is firm and well-shaped and sew up the gap.

3 Knit the arms (make two)

Using US 7 (4.5mm) needles and yarn A (brown), cast on 6 sts.
Work 5½in (14cm) in st st.
Bind (cast) off all sts.
Fold each piece in half widthwise and sew up one short seam and the long seam. Fill the arm with toy stuffing until it is well shaped—use the wrong end of a pencil to help push small bits of stuffing all the way to the end. Sew up the remaining short seam.

4 Knit the legs (make two)

Using US 7 (4.5mm) needles and yarn B (purple), cast on 11 sts.

Work in st st for two rows.

Change to yarn C (pink) and work 2 rows st st.

Continue straight in st st in this way, changing color every two rows until the legs measure 12in (30cm).

Bind (cast) off all sts and weave in the ends.

Fold each piece in half widthwise and sew it up and stuff it in the same way as you did for the arms, although you might need the wrong end of a knitting needle to push the stuffing right down the legs!

5 Sew the body together

Sew the head, arms, and legs to the body, with the arms about ½in (1cm) down from the top of the body and the legs attached to the bottom seam of the body. Use overstitches and match up the seam edges to sew them together.

6 Knit the dress front

Using US 7 (4.5mm) needles and yarn D (green), cast on 28 sts.

Work 6 rows st st.

Row 7: K2tog, knit to last 2sts, k2tog.

Row 8: K2tog, knit to last 2sts, k2tog.

Work 6 rows st st.

Row 15: K2tog, knit to last 2sts,k2tog.

Row 16: K2tog, knit to last 2sts, k2tog.

Continue straight until work measures 6¼in (16cm).

Bind (cast) off all sts.

Knit the dress back in the same way.

7 Knit the pocket

Using US 7 (4.5mm) needles and yarn C (pink), cast on 9 sts.

Row 1: Purl.

Row 2: Inc1, knit to last st, inc1. (11 sts)

Repeat the last two rows once more. (13 sts)

Work 5 rows st st.

Bind (cast) off all sts.

8 Finish the dress

Hold the dress up against the doll and mark where the armholes need to be with pins. Sew up the sides of the dress stopping where you have put the pins. Stitch a couple of stitches in one shoulder but leave the other shoulder unstitched.

9 Sew the pocket to the front of the dress using yarn B (purple) and overstitches. Sew some buttons to the top of the dress—you can slip a piece of cardstock inside the dress to stop you sewing through to the other side! Fit the dress onto the doll and sew up the shoulder seam.

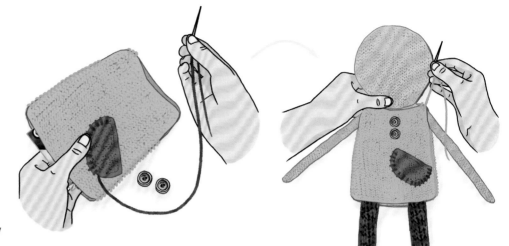

10 Make the hair
Cut 12 lengths of yarn B (purple), 49in (124cm) long. Fold the strands in half to find the center and then safety pin the center to the top of your doll's head. Thread the darning needle with yarn C (pink) and a little way to the left of the safety pin stitch over and over the strands of thread to make a pink stripe. Now do the same a little way to the right of the safety pin so that the stripes match. Remove the safety pin. Split one side of the hair into 3 sections with 4 strands of yarn in each section. Braid (plait) to the end, tying a knot at the bottom to stop it coming undone. Do the same for the other side.

11 Add the eyes and mouth
Sew on buttons for eyes. Draw around something round, like a button or cotton bobbin, onto the pink felt and cut out the circles, then sew them on with a sewing needle and thread for rosy cheeks. Embroider a smiley mouth in yarn with lots of straight stitches over each other.

Templates

All the templates provided here are at full size, so can be photocopied or traced as they are.

Little bear hat p28

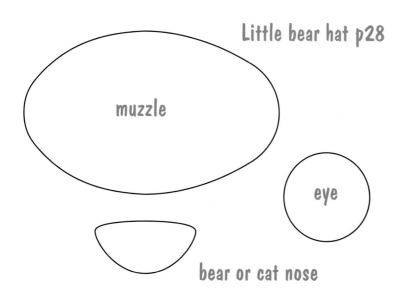

muzzle

eye

bear or cat nose

Animal scarves p36

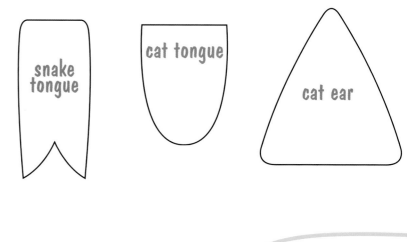

snake tongue

cat tongue

cat ear

Pirate flag p114

skull

bone

Suppliers and resources

Dummy you'll collect lots of materials from the outdoors for these projects, here are some links to places that sell craft and gardening materials and equipment.Dummy

USA

Debbie Bliss
Sirdar
Sublime
Knitting Fever Inc.
PO Box 336
315 Bayview Ave
Amityville
NY 11701
Tel: 516-546-3600
www.knittingfever.com

Rowan Yarns
Regia
Westminster Fibers Inc.
4 Townsend West
Suite 8
Nashua
NH 03063
Tel: 800-445-9276
www.westminsterfibers.com

Patons
Coats & Clark
Consumer Services
P.O. Box 12229
Greenville
SC 29612-0229
Tel: 800-648-1479
www.coatsandclark.com

Purl (shop)
459 Broome Street
New York
NY 10013
Tel: 212-420-8796
www.purlsoho.com

Downtown Yarns (shop)
45 Avenue A
New York
NY 10009
Tel: 212-995-5991
www.downtownyarns.com

Canada

Patons
320 Livingstone Avenue
South
Listowel
Ontario N4W 3H3
Tel: 1-888-368-8401
www.patonsyarns.com

Debbie Bliss
Regia
Rowan yarns
Sirdar
Sublime
Diamond Yarns Ltd
155 Martin Ross Avenue
Unit 3
Toronto
Ontario M3J 2L9
Tel: 416-736-6111
www.diamondyarn.com

UK

Sirdar Spinning Ltd.
Flanshaw Lane
Wakefield
West Yorkshire WF2 9ND
United Kingdom
Tel: 01924 371501
www.sirdar.co.uk

Debbie Bliss
Designer Yarns
Unit 8-10 Newbridge
Industrial Estate
Pitt Street
Keighley
West Yorkshire BD21 4PQ
Tel: 01535 664222
www.designeryarns.uk.com

Rowan Yarns
Green Lane Mill
Holmfirth
West Yorkshire HD9 2DX
Tel: 01484 681881
www.knitrowan.com

Patons

Coats Crafts UK
Green Lane Mill
Holmfirth
West Yorkshire HD9 2DX
Tel: 01484 681881
www.coatscrafts.co.uk

Loop (shop)

15 Camden Passage
Islington
London N1 8EA
Tel: 020 7288 1160
www.loopknitting.com

Get Knitted (shop)

39 Brislington Hill
Brislington
Bristol BS4 5BE
Tel: 0117 3005211
www.getknitted.com

International

Rico Yarns

RICO DESIGN GmbH & Co.
KG Industriestrasse 19 - 23
33034 Brakel
Germany
+49 52 72602-0
www.ricodesign.de

BC Garn

BC Garn Aps,
Elbow 56A
DK — 6000 Kolding
Denmark
+45 75 89 73 84
www.bcgarn.dk

Index

A
abbreviations 19

B
baby ball 108—9
backstitch 18
badge/brooch 56—7, 102—3
ballet slippers 67—9
basket, toy 97—9
bear hat 28—31, 124
belt, tassel 70—2
bind off 11
blanket, patchwork 84—7
blanket stitch 18
bows, brooch/hairgrip 56—7
buttons 8
    decorative 60—1
    sewing on 17

C
casting off 11
casting on 9
cat scarf 36—7, 124
caterpillar doorstop 90—3
chain stitch 18
color, changing 14
cowl 22—3
cozy knits 21—53
crochet hook 8, 14
cross stitch 17
cushions 88—9, 94—6
cute alien 117—19

D
darning needle 8, 15
decreasing 13, 19
doctor's stethoscope 106—7
doorstop, caterpillar 90—3
dropped stitches 14

E
earmuffs 24—7
embroidery stitches 17—18
ends, weaving in 15

F
fastening off 11
finger knitting 16, 64, 116
fingerless mitts 32—3
finishing touches 17
flat seam 15
French knitting 8, 17, 106—7
French knot 18
fun knits 100—23

G
garter stitch 12
gauge 13

H
hairgrips, bows 56—7
hats 28—31, 34—5, 38—41,
    44—7, 51—3
hearts 73—5, 88—9
home knits 80—99
hot-water bottle cover 82—3

I
increasing (inc1) 13, 19

K
key ring charm, heart 73—5
knit stitch 10, 13, 19
knitting
    finishing off 11, 17
    gauge/tension 13
    getting started 9
    needles 8
    stitch patterns 12
    stitches 10—11

L
ladybug buddies 104—5
legwarmers 58—9

M
materials 8, 126—7
mitts 32—3, 48—50
monster hat 51—3
moss stitch 12
mouse mittens 48—50
MP3 cover 62—3

N
necklace, pompom 64—6
needles 8

O
octopus hat 44—7
overstitch 15

P
panda hat 38—41
patchwork blanket 84—7
pattern, following 19
pencil case 76—9
phone cover 62—3
picking up stitches 14
pillows 88—9, 94—6
pirate flag 114—16, 125
pompom
    making 8, 16, 64—5
    necklace 64—6
    scarf 42—3
projects, difficulty 7
purl stitch 10, 13, 19

R
rag doll 120—3
rainbow earflap hat 34—5
rib stitch 11, 12
running stitch 17

S
scarves 22—3, 36—7, 42—3,
    70
scissors 8
seams 15
seed stitch 12
sewing needles 8
sewing up 15
shaping 13
sheriff's star badge 102—3
slip knot 9, 19
slip slip knit (ssk) 13, 19
snake scarf 36—7, 124
star, decoration/badge 102—3
stitch holder 8
stitches
    abbreviations 19
    embroidery 17—18
    knitting 10—11
    patterns 12
    picking up 14
stockinette/stocking stitch 12
stuffing 8
stylish knits 54—79
suppliers 126—7

T
tassel belt 70—2
techniques 9—19
teddy bear 70, 110—13
tension 13
toys
    baby ball 108—9
    cute alien 117—19
    doctor's stethoscope 106—7
    ladybug buddies 104—5
    pirate flag 114—16, 125
    rag doll 120—3
    stuffing 8
    teddy bear 110—13
    toy basket 97—9

Y
changing/joining 14
holding 9
suppliers 126—7
types 8
weaving in ends 15

Z
zigzag pillow 94—6

Acknowledgments

PROJECT MAKERS

Claire Montgomerie:
pp 22-23, 24-25, 26-27,
32-33, 34-35, 36-37, 42-43,
48-49, 56-57, 58-59, 60-61,
62-63, 64-66, 67-69, 70-72,
73-75, 76-77, 78-79, 82-83,
84-87, 88-89, 90-93, 94-96,
97-99, 102-103, 104-105,
106-107, 108-109, 110-113,
114-116, 117-119, 120-123

Fiona Goble:
pp 28-31, 38-41, 44-47, 51-53

PHOTOGRAPHY

Terry Benson:
pp 22-23, 24-25, 26-27,
28-31, 32-33, 34-35, 36-37,
38-41, 44-47, 48-49, 51-53,
56-57, 58-59, 60-61, 62-63,
64-66, 67-69, 70-72, 82-83,
84-87, 88-89, 90-93, 94-96,
102-103, 104-105, 106-107,
108-109, 110-113, 117-119,
120-123

Martin Norris:
pp 22-23, 24-25, 26-27,
32-33, 34-35, 36-37, 48-49,
56-57, 58-59, 60-61, 62-63,
64-66, 67-69, 70-72, 82-83,
84-87, 88-89, 90-93, 94-96,
102-103, 104-105, 106-107,
108-109, 110-113, 117-119,
120-123

Emma Mitchell:
pp 28-31, 38-41, 42-43,
44-47, 51-53, 73-75, 76-79,
97-99, 114-116

Penny Wincer:
28-31, 38-41, 44-47, 51-53

STYLIST

Sophie Martell:
pp 42-43, 73-75, 76-79,
97-99, 114-116